Since ancient times, people have been inventing different ways of getting around. There are things that travel **across land, through water** and **up in the air.**

In this book, there are **exactly 1000** vehicles, from folding bicycles and horse-drawn carriages to spacecraft that are exploring our solar system and beyond.

The pictures are **not drawn to scale.** For example, the ships on page 13 are actually 70 times bigger than the cars on page 9.

Every picture is labelled with its name, and there's a list of all the names at the back of the book.

USBORNE

1000 THINGS THAT GO

Illustrated by Gabriele Antonini

Researched and edited by Rachel Wilkie and Hannah Wood
Designed by Matt Durber
Cover design by Yasmin Faulkner

Expert advice
Alan Barnes, Alexi Holden-Crowther, Andrew Gaved, Anthony Coulls, Ben Holden-Crowther, Brian Voakes, Colin Jarman, David Cousins, David Coxon, David Willey, Doug Hilton, Elfan Ap Rees, James Wilkie, John Robinson, Neil Johnson-Symington, Nicholas Leach, Richard Thompson, Sam Collins, Stephen Courtney, Steve Fowler

Contents

In the city
Page 5

Emergency vehicles
Page 6

At the airport
Page 7

On holiday
Page 8

Lots of cars
Page 9

Racing
Page 10

Motorbikes
Page 11

Famous ships
Page 11

Historic ships
Page 12

Big ships
Page 13

Sailing boats
Page 14

In the water
Page 15

In the sky
Page 16

Fighter planes
Page 17

Tanks and armoured vehicles Page 18

Battleships and submarines Page 19

Military helicopters Page 20

Diggers and excavators Page 20

At the building site Page 21

Trucks Page 22

On the farm Page 23

Old-fashioned things that go Page 24

Steam locomotives Page 25

Trains and trams Page 26

Pedalling, pushing and pulling Page 27

Tricky terrain Page 28

Rockets Page 29

In space Page 30

Unusual things that go Page 31

Index Page 32

In the city

London Underground train

Boda-boda bicycle

Bendy bus

Black cab

Delivery van

School bus

Paris Metro train

Post van

Powered wheelchair

Cyclo

Moped

Van

Electric bicycle

New York Subway train

Double-decker bus

Berlin U-Bahn train

Matatu

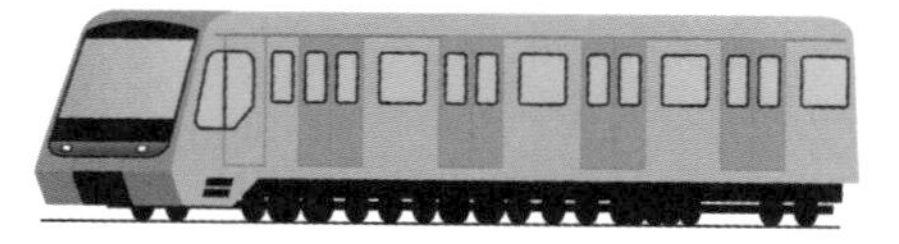
Hong Kong Mass Transit Railway train

Mobility scooter

Bike-share bicycle

Trisikad taxi

Thai tuk-tuk

Waste disposal truck

Tokyo Metro train

Folding bicycle

Water taxi

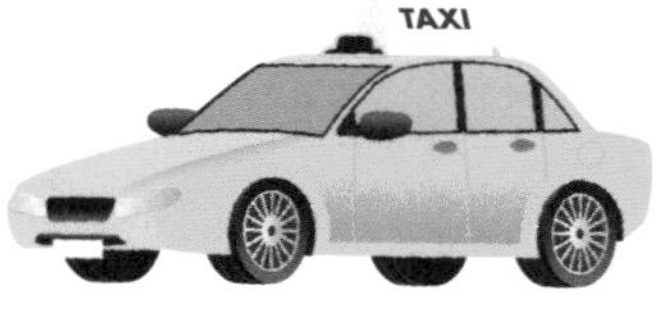

Yellow taxi

Pizza delivery scooter

Motor scooter

Indian auto-rickshaw

Streetcar

Utility bicycle

Minibus

Street sweeper

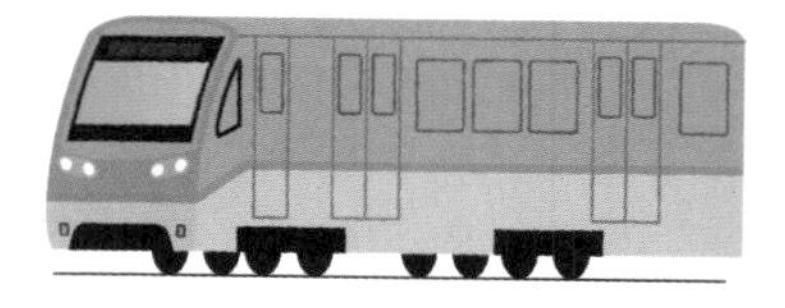
Moscow Metro train

Emergency vehicles

Fire truck

Emergency doctor car

Blood service car

Ambulance

Cave rescue vehicle

Lifeboat

Police dog van

Police van

Search and rescue vehicle

Lifeguard patrol vehicle

Mountain rescue vehicle

Veterinary ambulance

Bomb disposal vehicle

All-terrain fire vehicle

Rapid response ambulance car

Fire motorbike

Ambulance motorbike

Police motorbike

Police bicycle

Traffic police car

Mines rescue vehicle

Motorsport rescue car

Police patrol car

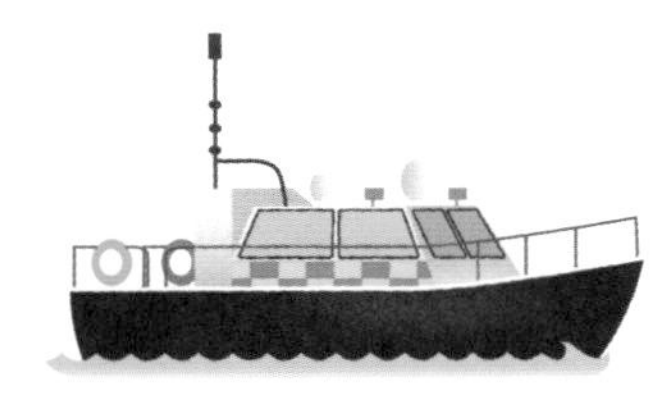

Police boat

Surf rescue boat

Lifeguard boat

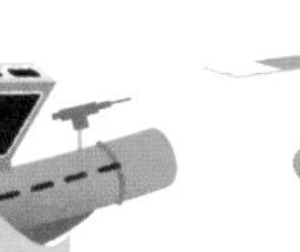

Coastguard boat

Coastguard helicopter

Fire-fighting helicopter

Fire boat

Rescue helicopter

Air ambulance

Police helicopter

Fire-fighting water bomber

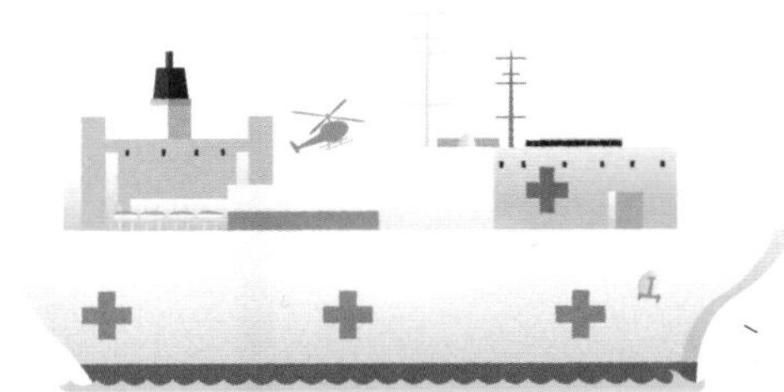

Hospital ship

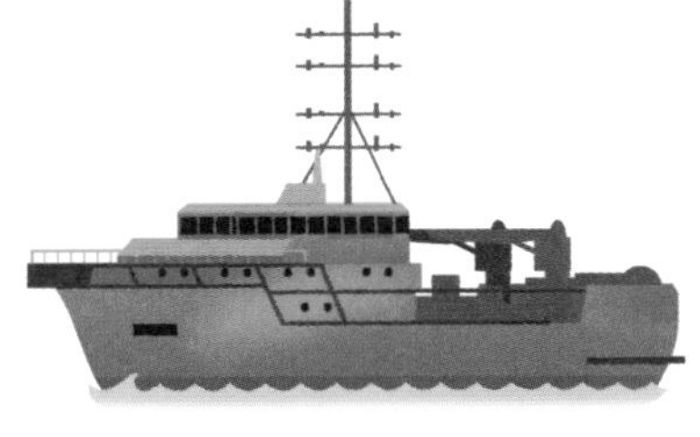

Emergency rescue ship

Armoured special forces vehicle

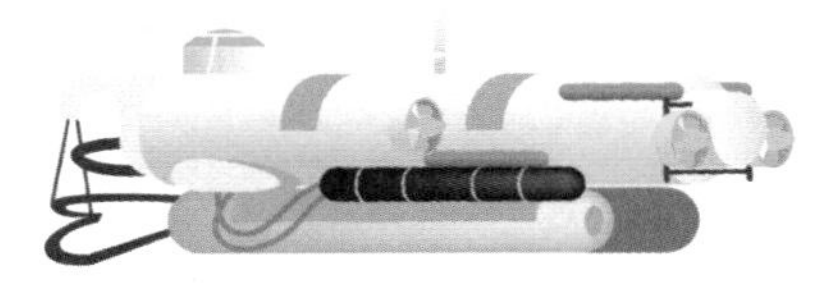

Submarine rescue vehicle

At the airport

Security vehicle

Baggage truck

'Follow me' truck

Double-deck plane

De-icing truck

Airside transfer bus

Airport caddy

Front-entry cargo plane

Rear-entry cargo plane

Airport shuttle train

Airport maintenance truck

Customs vehicle

Four-engined jet plane

Runway sweeper

Airport fire appliance

Mobile baggage conveyor

Cargo loader

Shuttle bus

Regional jet

Turboprop plane

Corporate jet

Three-engined jet plane

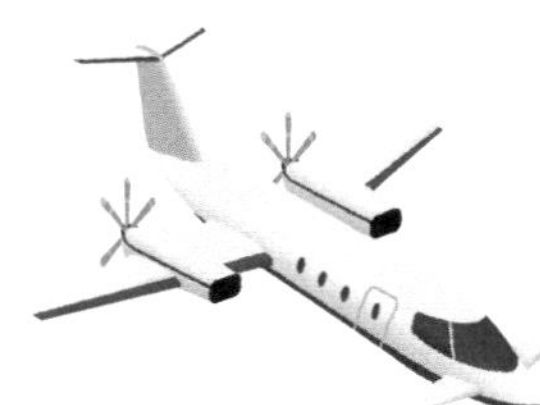
Twin-piston aircraft

Jumbo jet

Twin-engined plane

Airport fuel truck

Lavatory service vehicle

Air start unit

Aircraft tug

Jetliner

Aircraft catering truck

Ground power unit

Boarding stair truck

Passenger lift

Side-entry cargo plane

On holiday

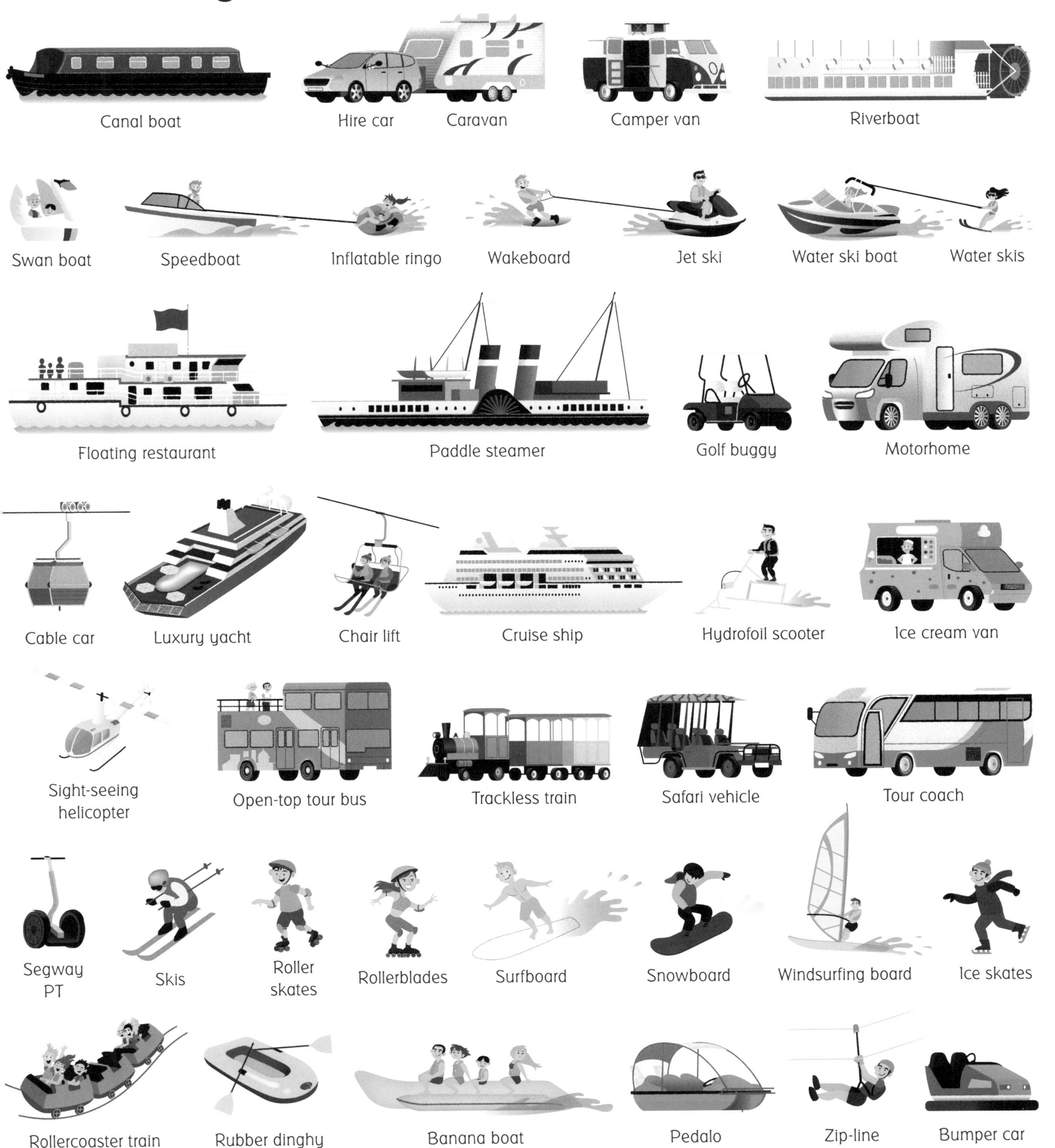

Canal boat
Hire car
Caravan
Camper van
Riverboat
Swan boat
Speedboat
Inflatable ringo
Wakeboard
Jet ski
Water ski boat
Water skis
Floating restaurant
Paddle steamer
Golf buggy
Motorhome
Cable car
Luxury yacht
Chair lift
Cruise ship
Hydrofoil scooter
Ice cream van
Sight-seeing helicopter
Open-top tour bus
Trackless train
Safari vehicle
Tour coach
Segway PT
Skis
Roller skates
Rollerblades
Surfboard
Snowboard
Windsurfing board
Ice skates
Rollercoaster train
Rubber dinghy
Banana boat
Pedalo
Zip-line
Bumper car

Lots of cars

Kei car
Bubble car
Hardtop
3-door hatchback
Classic car
Hybrid car
Sports car
Muscle car
Multi-purpose vehicle
City car
Gullwing car
Kit car
Solar car
Supercar
Cabriolet
Four-wheel drive
Coupé
Electric car
5-door hatchback
Le Mans classic car
Crossover
Estate car
Roadster
Microcar
Hot hatch
Classic cabriolet
Luxury car
Track day car
Saloon car
Three-wheeler
Classic limousine
Stretch limousine

Racing

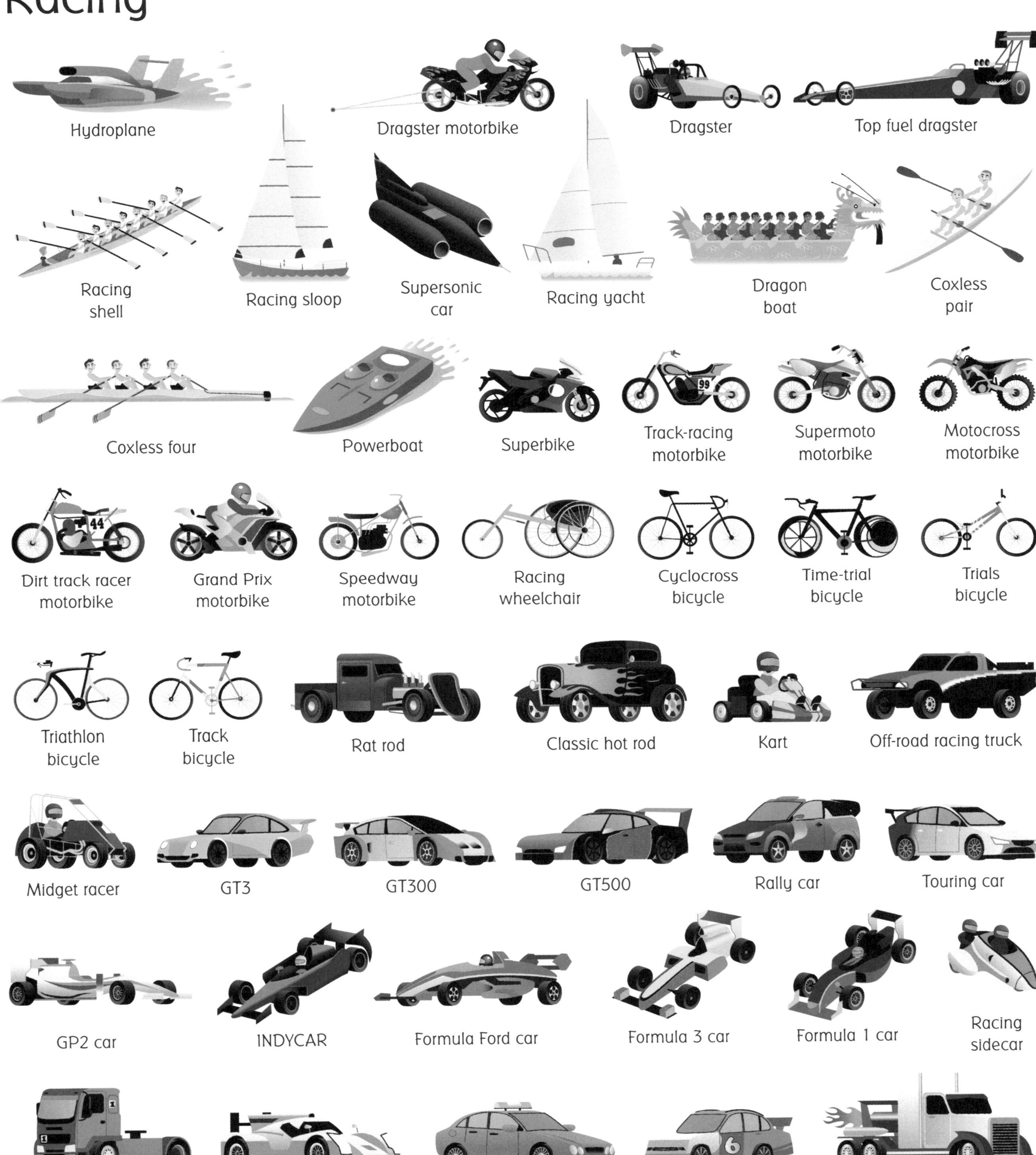

Hydroplane
Dragster motorbike
Dragster
Top fuel dragster
Racing shell
Racing sloop
Supersonic car
Racing yacht
Dragon boat
Coxless pair
Coxless four
Powerboat
Superbike
Track-racing motorbike
Supermoto motorbike
Motocross motorbike
Dirt track racer motorbike
Grand Prix motorbike
Speedway motorbike
Racing wheelchair
Cyclocross bicycle
Time-trial bicycle
Trials bicycle
Triathlon bicycle
Track bicycle
Rat rod
Classic hot rod
Kart
Off-road racing truck
Midget racer
GT3
GT300
GT500
Rally car
Touring car
GP2 car
INDYCAR
Formula Ford car
Formula 3 car
Formula 1 car
Racing sidecar
Racing truck
Le Mans prototype
Race safety car
Stockcar
Pro jet truck

Motorbikes

Street bike

Cruiser motorbike

Streamliner motorcycle

Road superbike

Universal Japanese motorcycle

Electric motorbike

Sport bike

Dual sport motorbike

Bobber

Rat bike

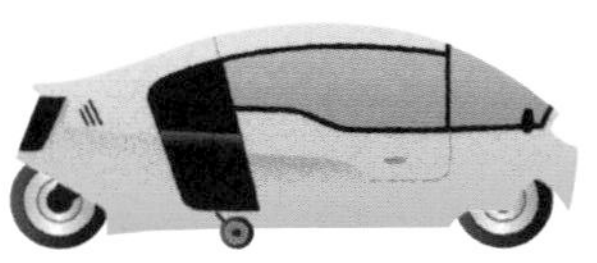
Cabin motorcycle

Touring motorbike

Mini chopper

Electric rocket drag bike

Motorcycle trike

Classic 1930s motorbike

Derny

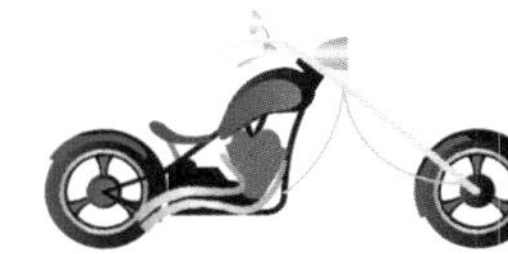
Chopper

Feet first motorcycle

Café racer

Streetfighter bike

Underbone

Enduro motorbike

Sport touring bike

Famous ships

HMS Bounty

Cutty Sark

HMS Sovereign of the Seas

Golden Hind

Mary Celeste

Bluenose

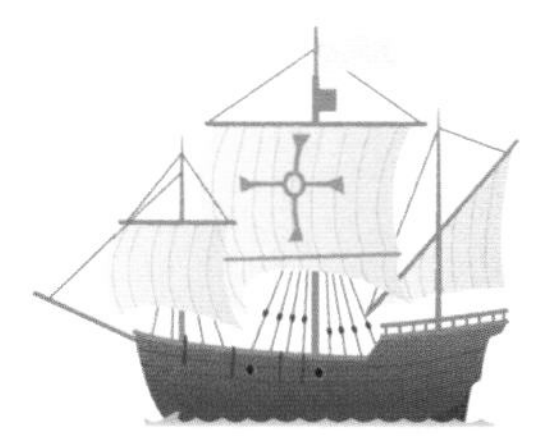
La Pinta

Mayflower

Nao Victoria

RMS Titanic

HMS Beagle

SS Central America

Thermopylae

Turbinia

Syracusia

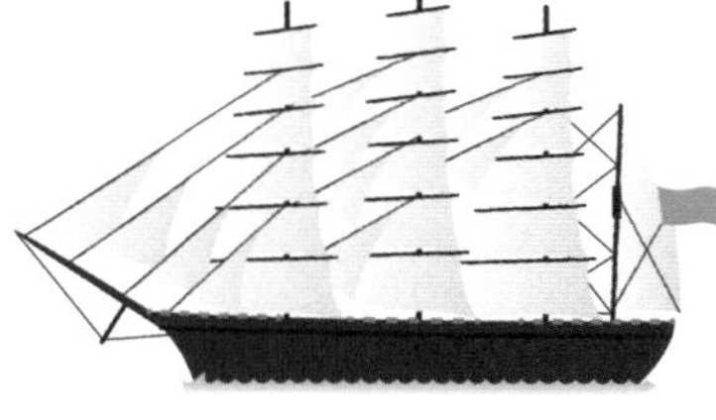
Great Republic

SS Savannah

Historic ships

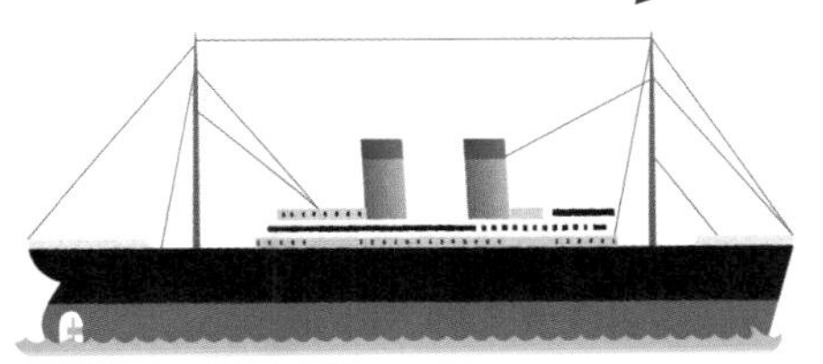
Passenger steamship

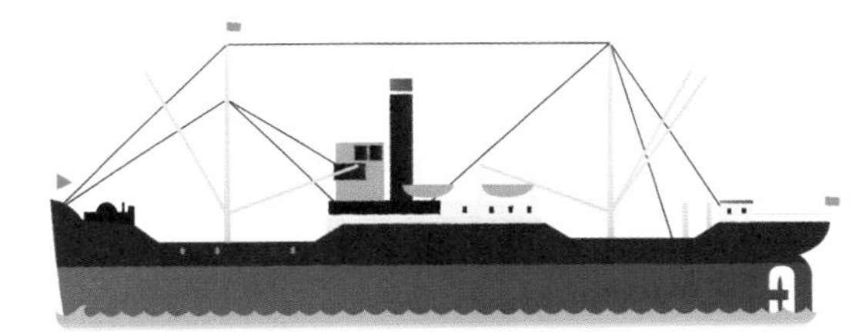
Tramp steamer

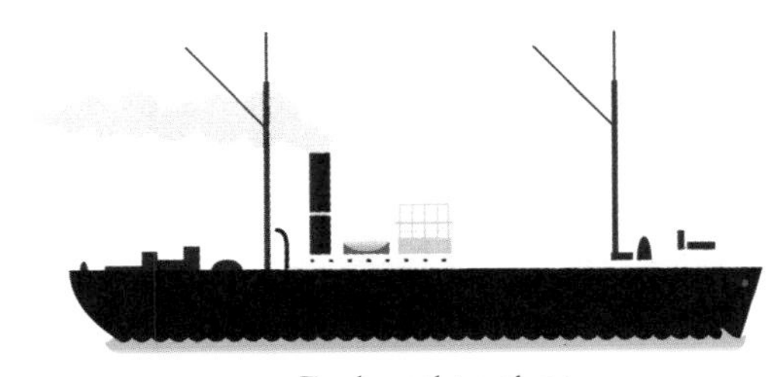
Early oil-tanker

Palace steamer

Snag boat

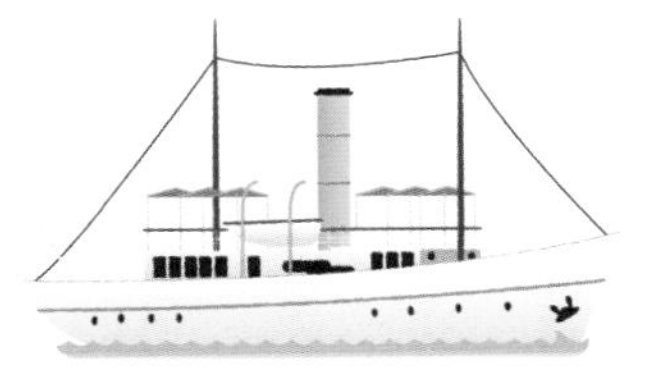
Steam yacht

Hickman sea sled

Galleon

Brig

Man-of-war

Blackwall frigate

Barque

Fluyt

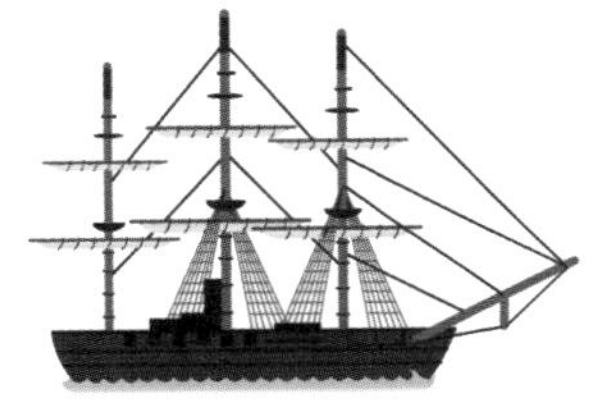
Screw barque

Baltimore clipper

Panokseon

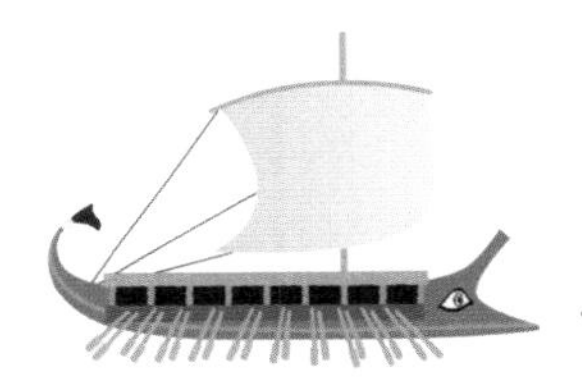
Penteconter

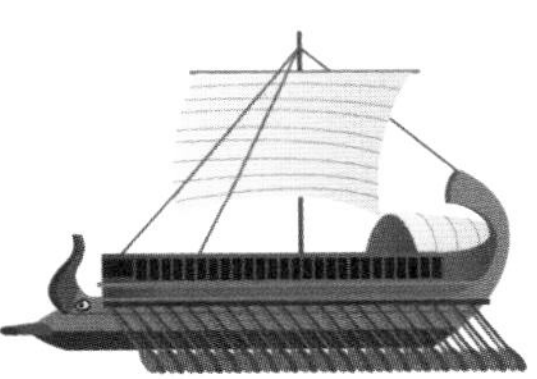
Dromond

Quinquereme

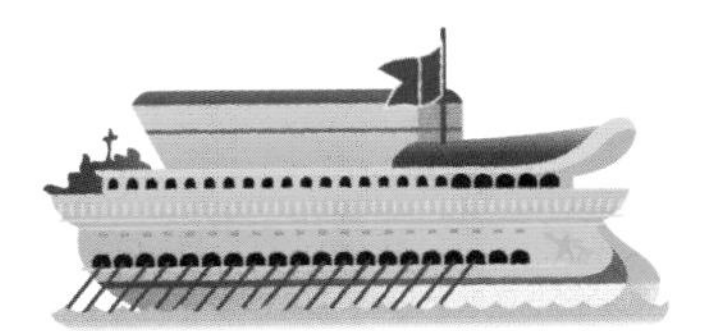
Bucentaur

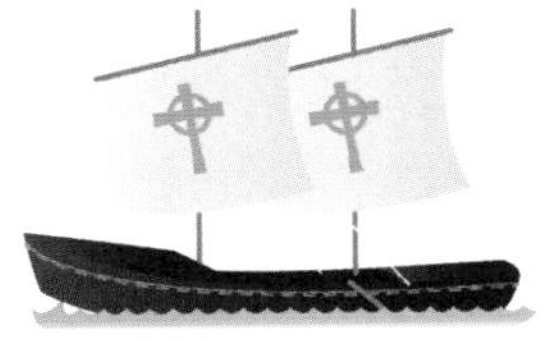
Currach

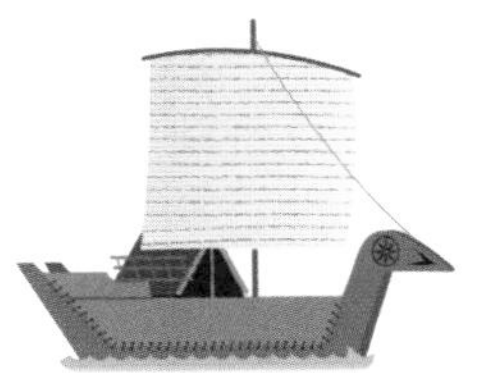
Mtepe

Turtle ship

Roman galley

Junk

Galleass

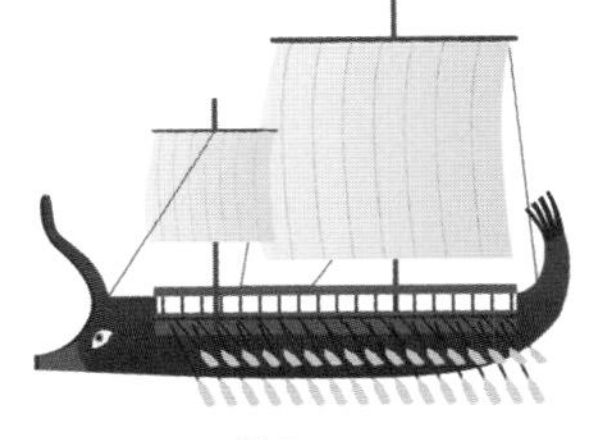
Trireme

Barquentine

Viking longship

Roman merchant ship

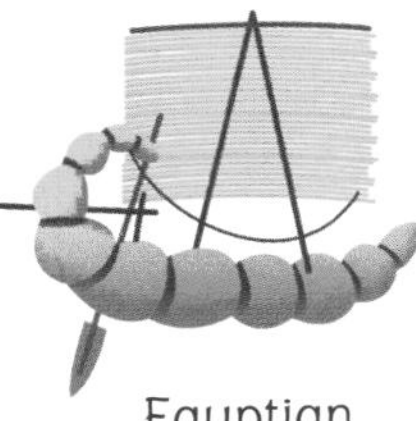
Egyptian papyrus boat

Cog

Caravel

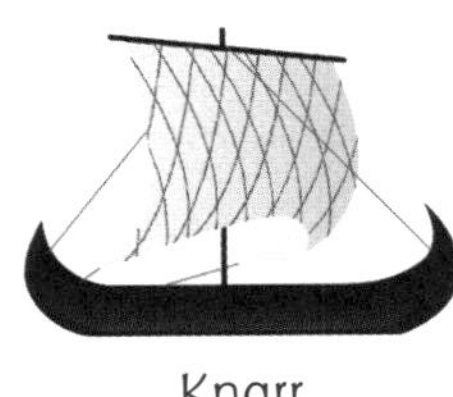
Knarr

Big ships

LNG tanker
Freight ferry
Fast ferry
Icebreaker
Cross Channel ferry
Great Lakes freighter
Aframax tanker
Articulated tugbarge
Crude oil tanker
Cable layer
X-bow support ship
Flo-flo ship
Flettner's rotor ship
Ro-pax ferry
Cargo liner
Chemical tanker
Supertanker
Product tanker
Crane ship
Shuttle tanker
Trinity House tender
Drillship
Tug
Panamax ship
Bulker
Chain ferry
Pipe-laying ship
Container ship
Factory trawler
Platform supply vessel
Merchant vessel
Suction dredger
Straight-decker
Heavy lift ship

Sailing boats

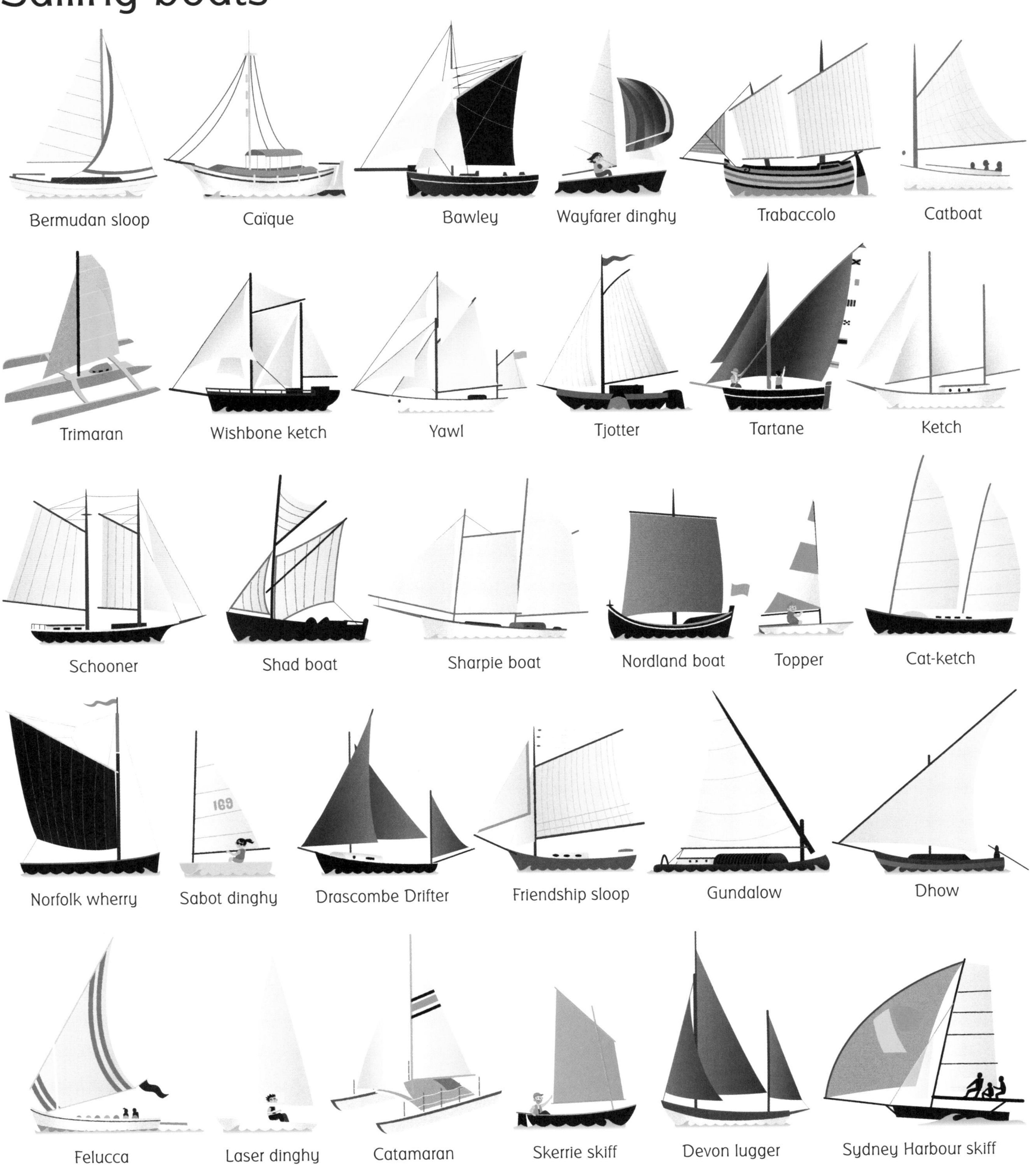

In the water

Float tube
Bow rider
Longtail boat
Pirogue
Bass boat
Bathtub boat
Cuddy boat
Kayak
Waka
Slipper launch
Flyak
Go-fast boat
Logboat
Midget submarine
Reed boat
Deep-submergence vehicle
Clyde puffer
Raft
Sailing yacht
Bilibili
Coble
Lighter barge
Shikara
Pontoon
Tarai bune
Masula boat
Pump boat
Umiak
Canoe
Pram boat
Flatboat
Fishing boat
Supercavitation boat
Hydrofoil
Houseboat
Bathyscaphe
Motor yacht
Jon boat
Sampan
Outrigger canoe
Very Slender Vessel
Recreational submarine
Coracle

In the sky

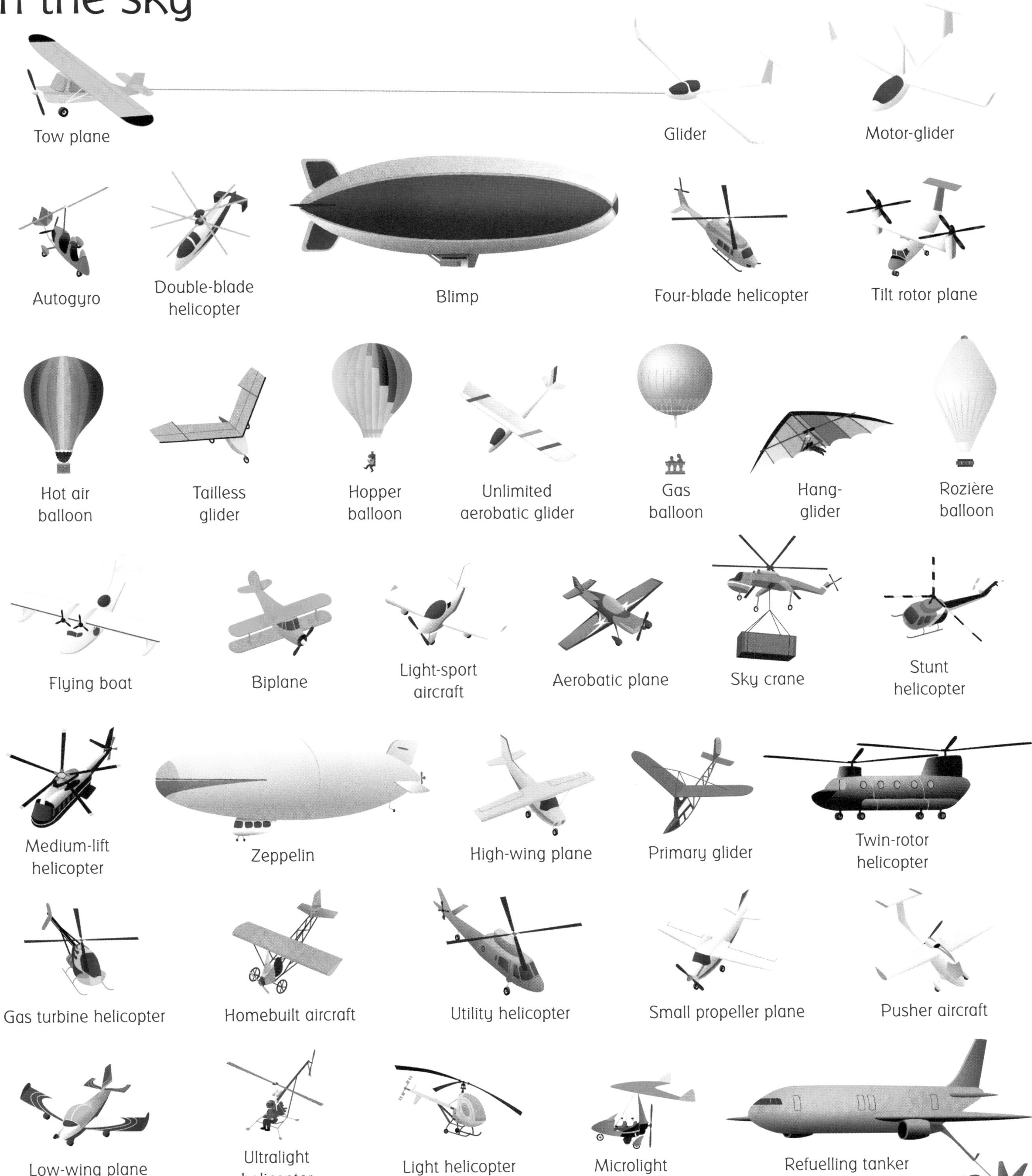

Tow plane
Glider
Motor-glider
Autogyro
Double-blade helicopter
Blimp
Four-blade helicopter
Tilt rotor plane
Hot air balloon
Tailless glider
Hopper balloon
Unlimited aerobatic glider
Gas balloon
Hang-glider
Rozière balloon
Flying boat
Biplane
Light-sport aircraft
Aerobatic plane
Sky crane
Stunt helicopter
Medium-lift helicopter
Zeppelin
High-wing plane
Primary glider
Twin-rotor helicopter
Gas turbine helicopter
Homebuilt aircraft
Utility helicopter
Small propeller plane
Pusher aircraft
Low-wing plane
Ultralight helicopter
Light helicopter
Microlight
Refuelling tanker

Fighter planes

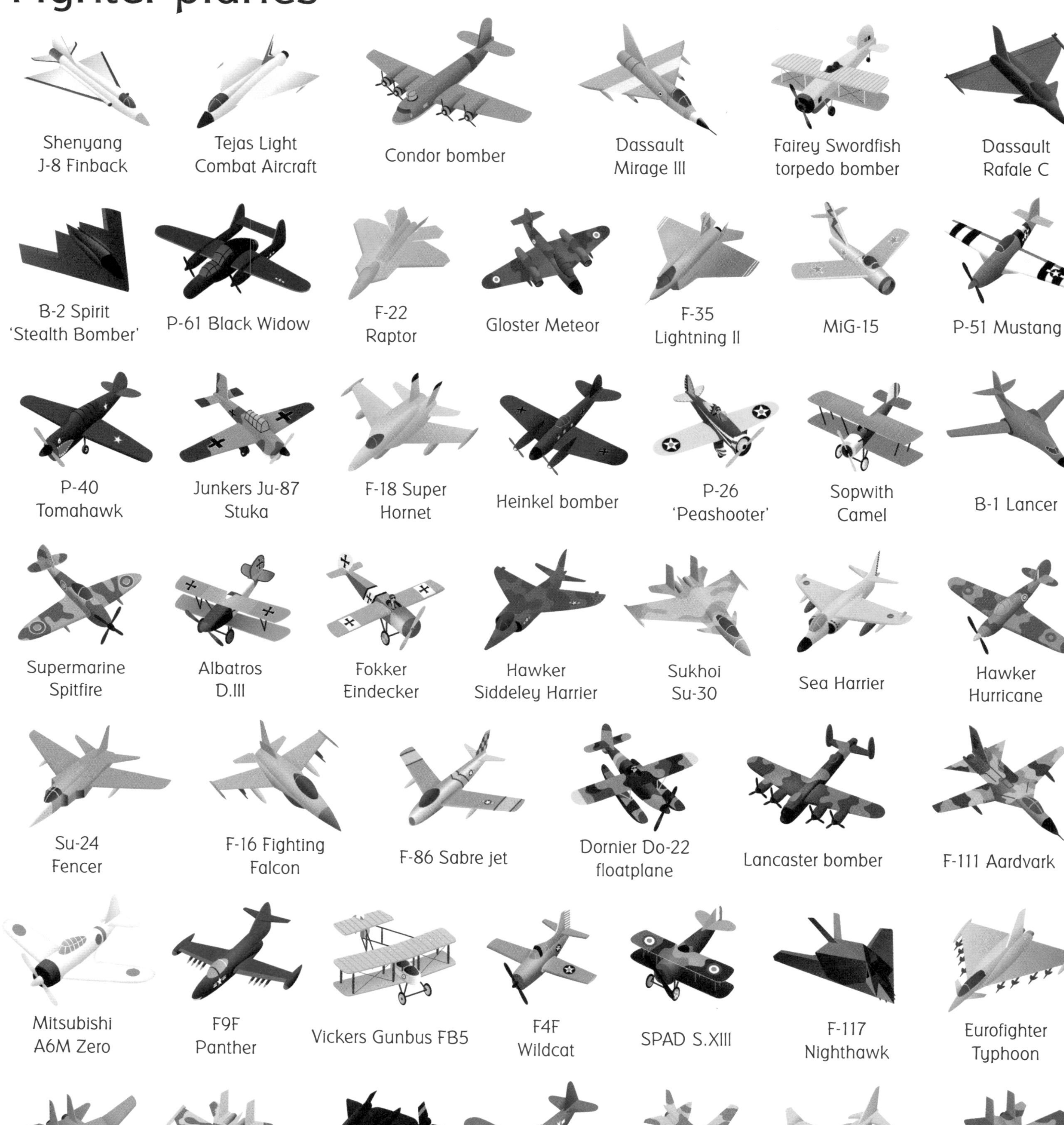

Tanks and armoured vehicles

Battleships and submarines

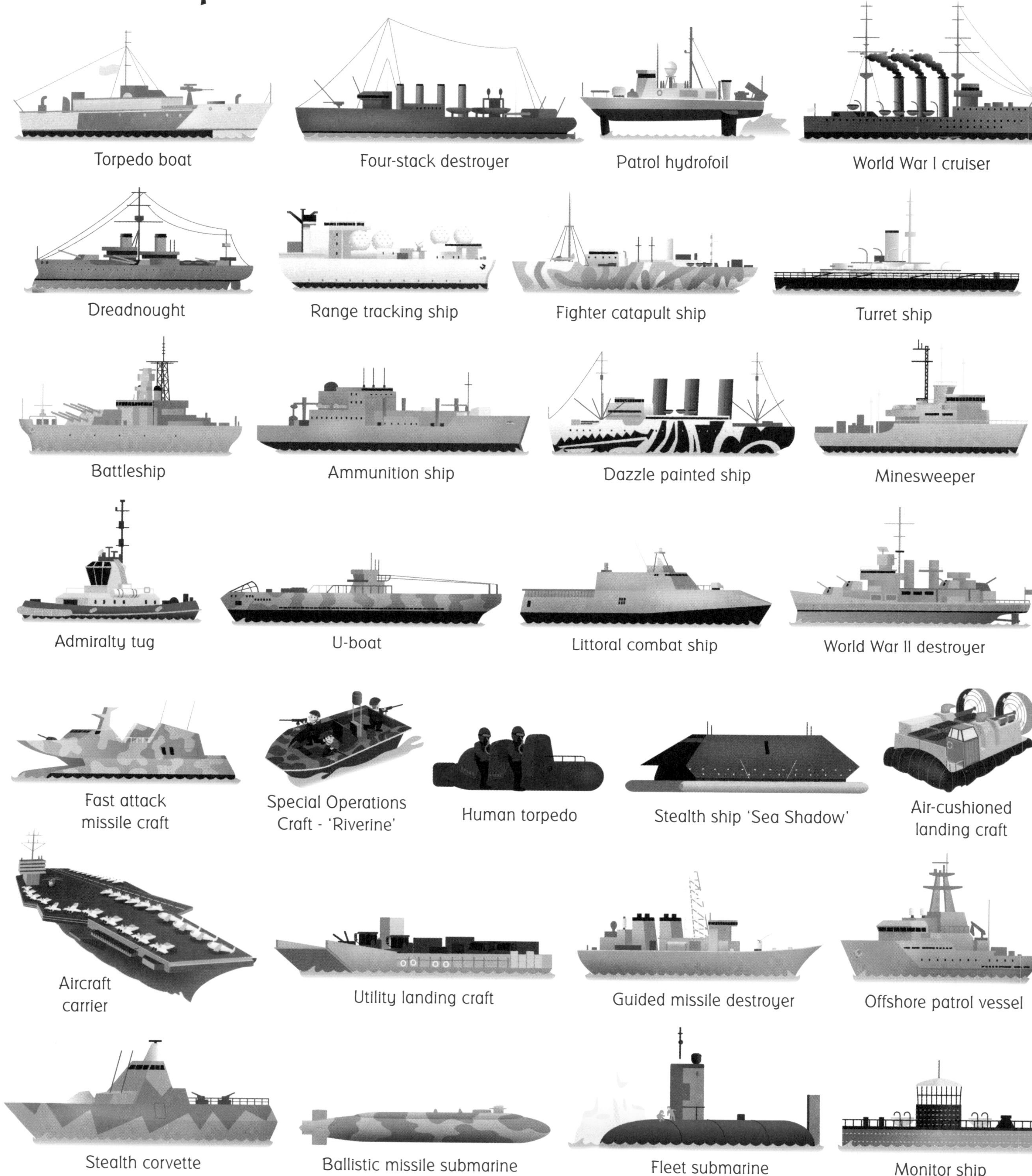

Military helicopters

Mi-24 Hind

AH-1 Cobra

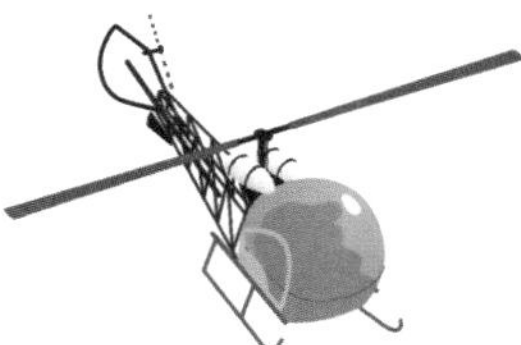
H-13 Sioux

AH-64 Apache

SH-3 Sea King

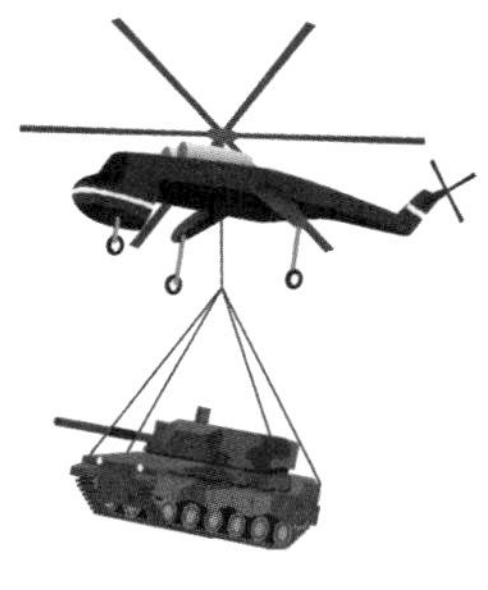
CH-54 Tarhe

UH-1 Iroquois

Focke-Achgelis Fa 223

Lynx Mk9A

MD 500 Defender

SA-330 Puma

H-34 Choctaw

UHT Tiger

KA-27 Helix

OH-6 Cayuse

Mi-10 Harke

CH-47 Chinook

UH-60 Black Hawk

Diggers and excavators

Trencher

Grader

Wheeled excavator

Bucket wheel excavator

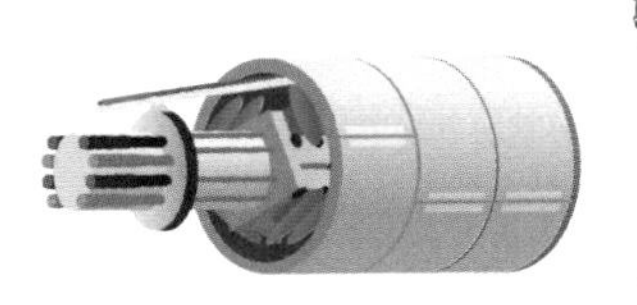
Tunnel boring machine

Roadheader

Suction excavator

Wheeled loader

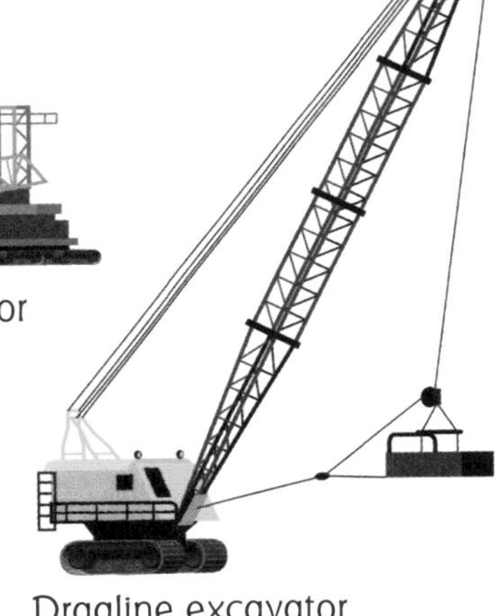
Dragline excavator

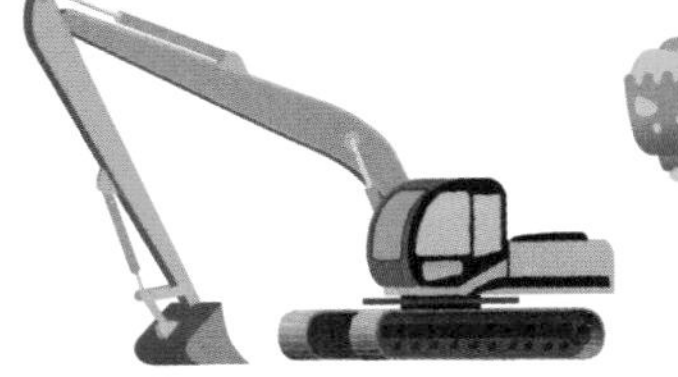
Long reach excavator

Backhoe loader

Giant loader

Auger excavator

Tracked excavator

Skid steer loader

Face-shovel

Site dumper

Grab excavator

Mini excavator

Bulldozer

At the building site

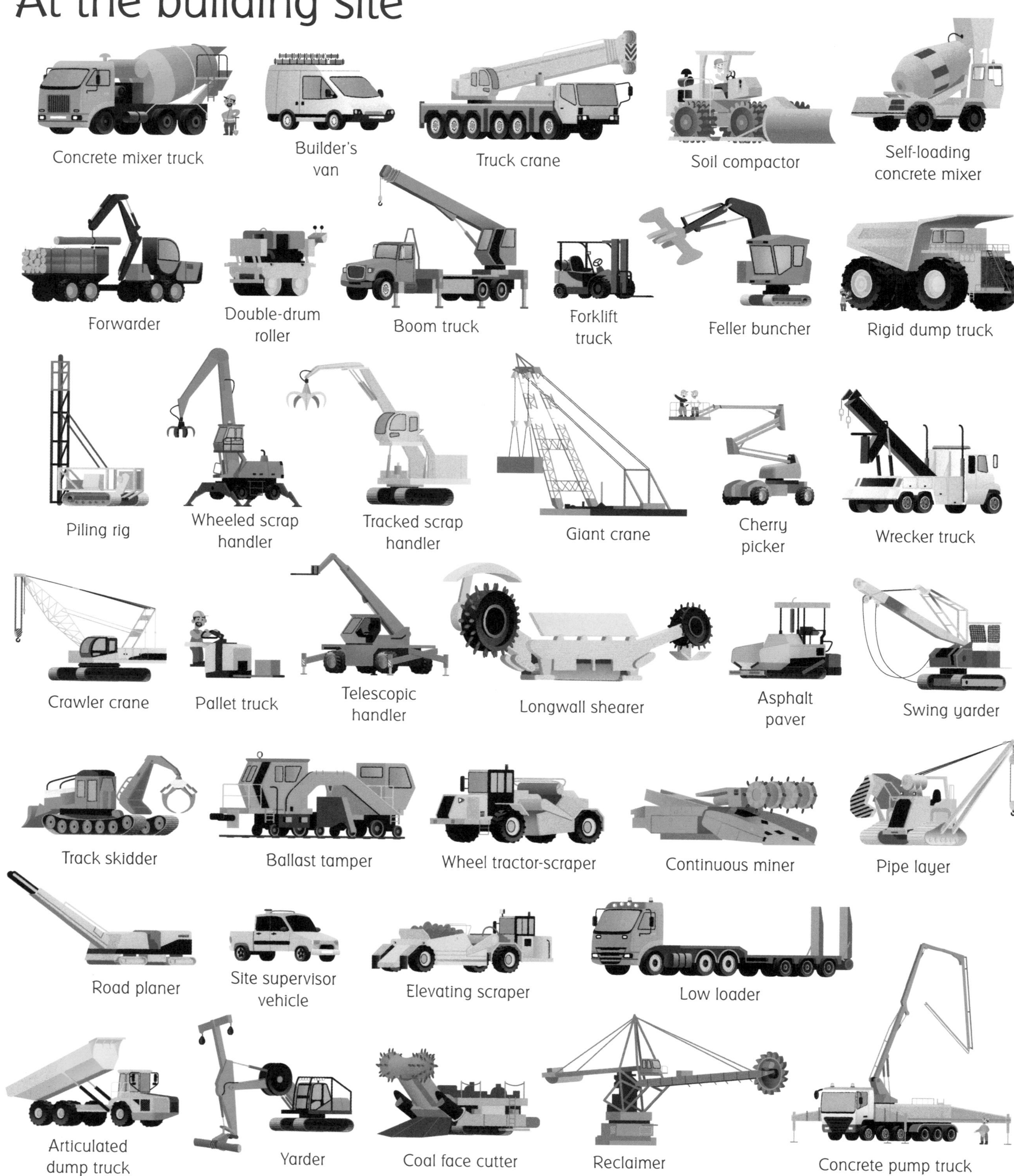
Concrete mixer truck
Builder's van
Truck crane
Soil compactor
Self-loading concrete mixer
Forwarder
Double-drum roller
Boom truck
Forklift truck
Feller buncher
Rigid dump truck
Piling rig
Wheeled scrap handler
Tracked scrap handler
Giant crane
Cherry picker
Wrecker truck
Crawler crane
Pallet truck
Telescopic handler
Longwall shearer
Asphalt paver
Swing yarder
Track skidder
Ballast tamper
Wheel tractor-scraper
Continuous miner
Pipe layer
Road planer
Site supervisor vehicle
Elevating scraper
Low loader
Articulated dump truck
Yarder
Coal face cutter
Reclaimer
Concrete pump truck

Trucks

Car transporter

Monster truck

Tipper truck

Scissor lift truck

Lattice boom truck crane

Delivery truck

Rigid truck

Catering truck

Container truck

Curtainsider

Mobile telescopic crane truck

Milk tanker

Logging truck

Highway maintenance truck

Big rig

Refuse collection truck

Gully emptier

Dekotora art truck

Heavy muscle truck

Snow-clearing truck

Dropside truck

Dry bulk tanker

Flatbed truck

Antenna transporter

Mail truck

Super-sized truck

Tow truck

Panel truck

Fuel tanker

Pick-up truck

Space Shuttle transporter truck

Tractor-trailer

All-terrain truck

Road-train

On the farm

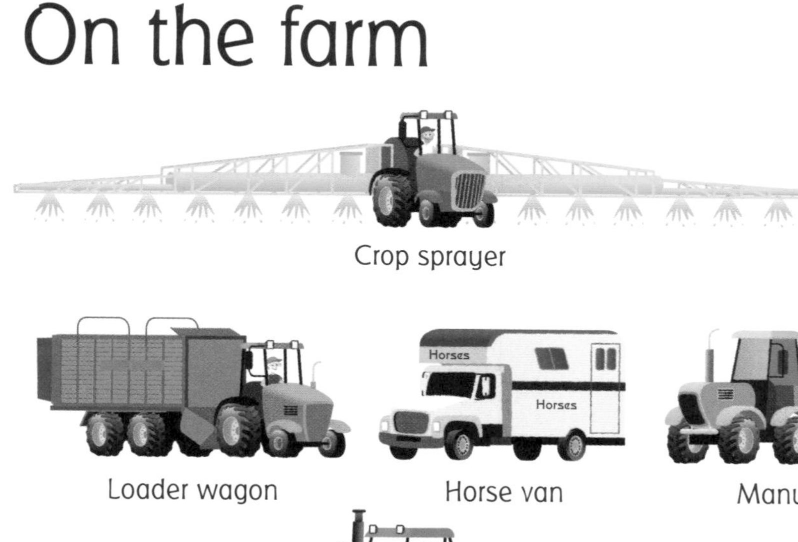

Crop sprayer

Crop duster

Disc harrow

Livestock truck

Loader wagon

Horse van

Manure spreader

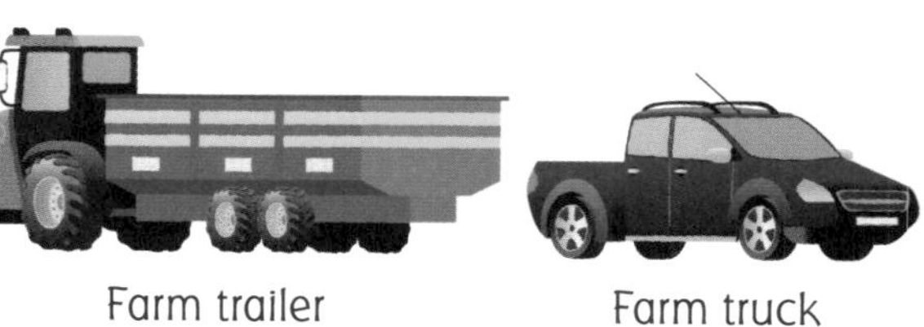

Farm trailer

Farm truck

Narrow tractor

Giant tractor

Baler

Six-wheeled tractor

Hay tedder

Garden tractor

Forage harvester

Crawler tractor

Tool-carrier tractor

Mini tractor

Post driver

Reversible tractor

Out-front tractor mower

Potato planter

Seed drill

Three-wheel tractor

Harvester

Allen scythe

Potato spinner

Rubber track tractor

Swather

Front loader tractor

Cultivator

Combine harvester

Flail mower

Root crop harvester

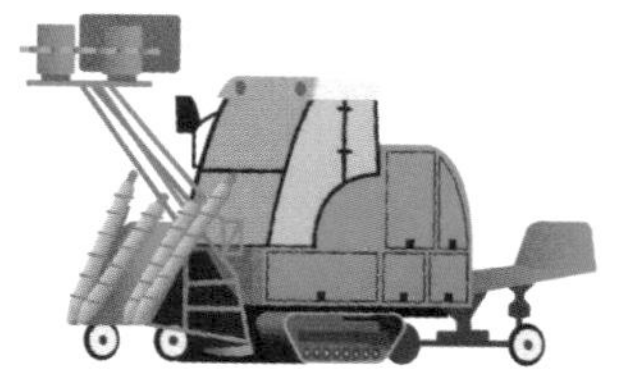

Sugar cane harvester

Walking tractor

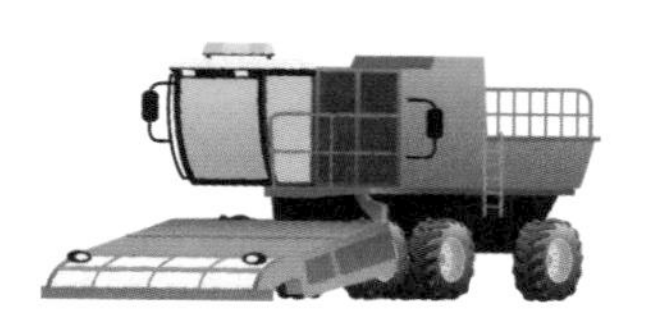

Bean harvester

High crop tractor

Broadcast seeder

Compact utility tractor

Grain cart

Cotton picker

Old-fashioned things that go

Mail coach

Clarence carriage

Brougham carriage

Surrey carriage

Conestoga wagon

Coal box buggy

Prairie schooner

Dray wagon

Farm wagon

Landau carriage

Chariot

Hansom cab

Wagonette

Concord stagecoach

Hop tug wagon

Dog cart

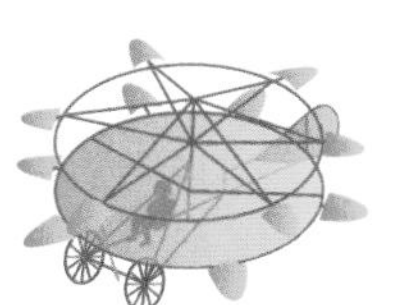
Ellehammer helicopter

Bristol Boxkite

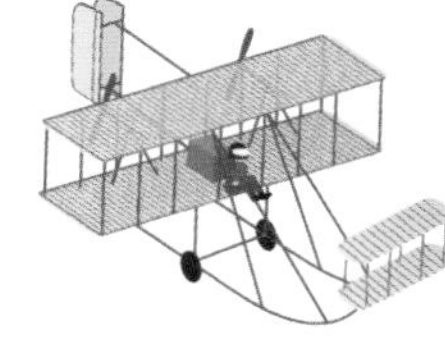
Wright Flyer III

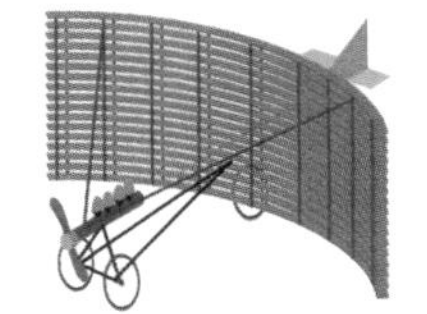
Phillips Multiplane

Berliner helicopter

Cornu helicopter

Montgolfier balloon

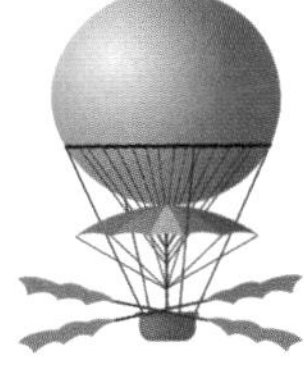
Blanchard's balloon

Charles' hydrogen balloon

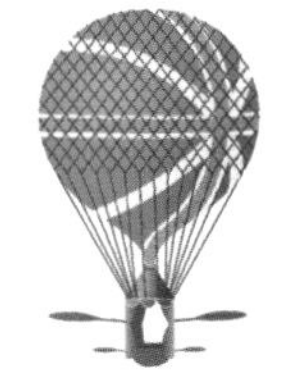
Lunardi balloon

Penny-farthing

Hobby-horse bicycle

Treadle bicycle

Sail wagon

Buckboard car

Omnibus

Steam car

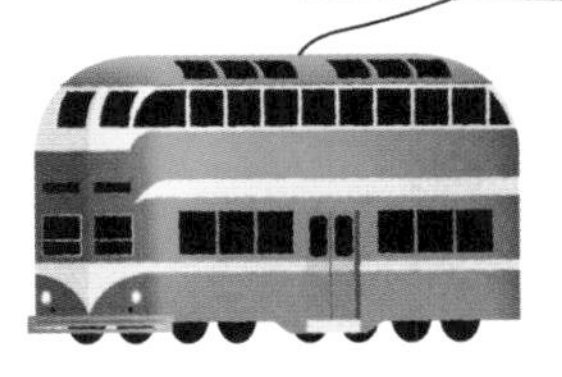
Trolleybus

Threshing machine

Daimler-Maybach motorcycle

Roper steam motorcycle

Ploughing engine

Steam tractor

Steamroller

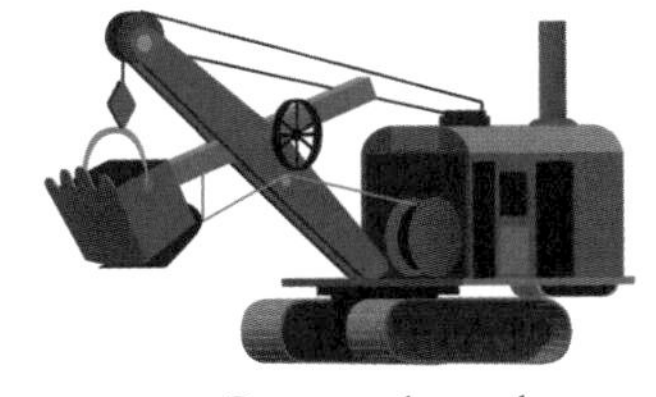
Steamshovel

Steam locomotives

2-2-2 locomotive

4-4-2 locomotive

Fireless locomotive

Articulated locomotive

Vertical boiler locomotive

Camelback locomotive

Duplex locomotive

Heilmann steam-electric locomotive

Rack-and-pinion locomotive

Cab forward locomotive

Saddle tank locomotive

Condensing steam locomotive

Fast goods locomotive

Geared steam locomotive

Freight steam locomotive

Underground steam train

Electric-steam locomotive

'Tom Thumb'

'Big Boy'

'Mallard'

'City of Truro'

'John Bull'

'The Leviathan'

'Puffing Billy'

'Stourbridge Lion'

'The Flying Scotsman'

'The Kingston Flyer'

'The Empire State Express'

'Adler'

'Fairy Queen Express'

Stephenson's 'Rocket'

Trevithick's locomotive

Trains and trams

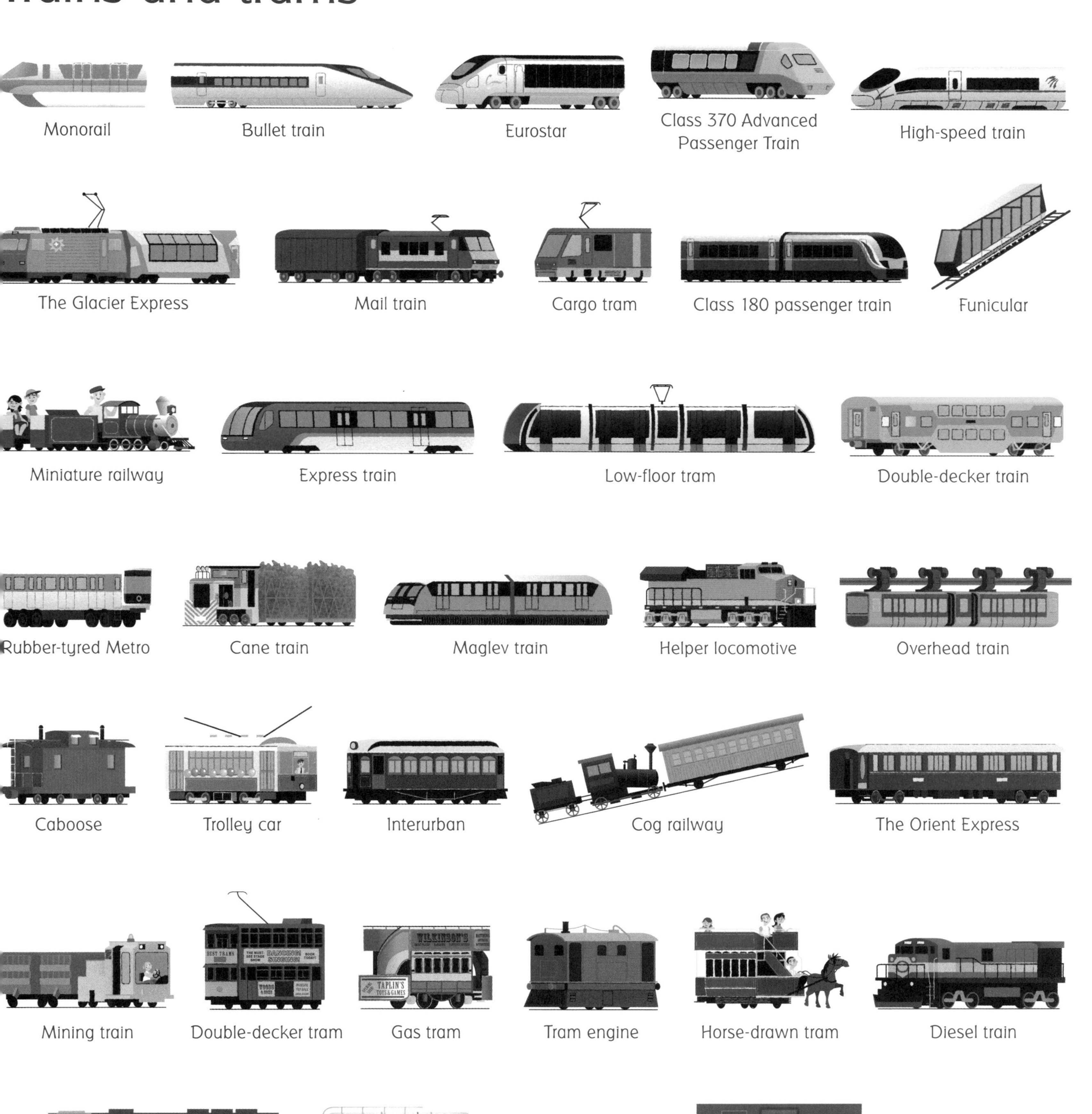

Freight train Tank wagon Open wagon Boxcar Flatcar

Pedalling, pushing and pulling

Banana board

Unicycle

Gondola

Recumbent bicycle

Conference bicycle

Lowrider bicycle

Child's tricycle

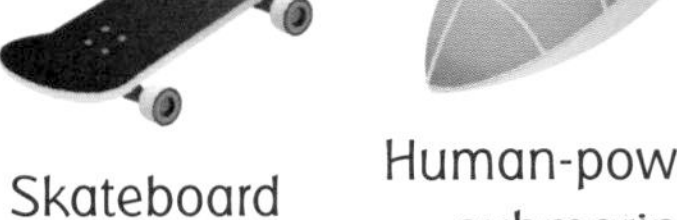
Skateboard

Human-powered submarine

Trailer cycle

Chopper-style bike

Freight bicycle

Rowing boat

Handcycle

BMX bicycle

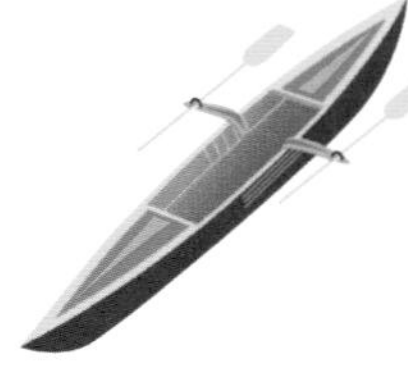
Sculling boat

Tandem

Porteur bicycle

Child trailer

Pedibus

Space hopper

Beach cruiser bicycle

Orange-crate scooter

Sociable bicycle

Small wheel bicycle

Kick scooter

Pogo stick

Bicycle rickshaw

Dekochari art bicycle

Longboard skateboard

Wave board

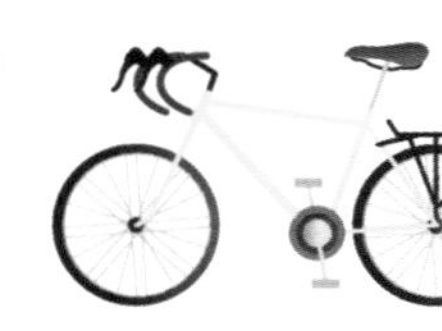
Touring bicycle

Velomobile

Wheelchair

Quadricycle

Hydro-bike

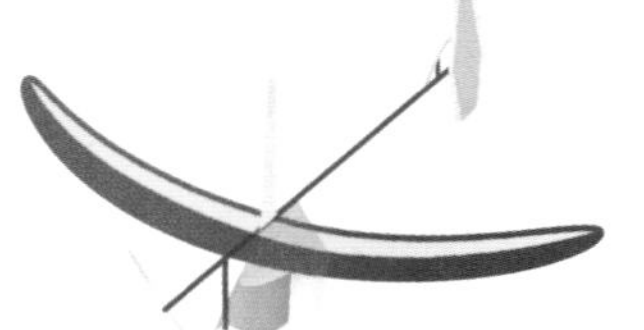
Human-powered aircraft

Micro scooter

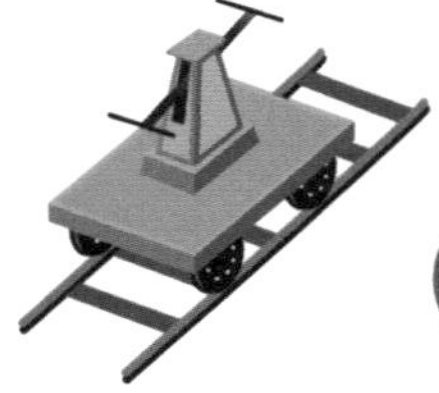
Handcar

Mountain bicycle

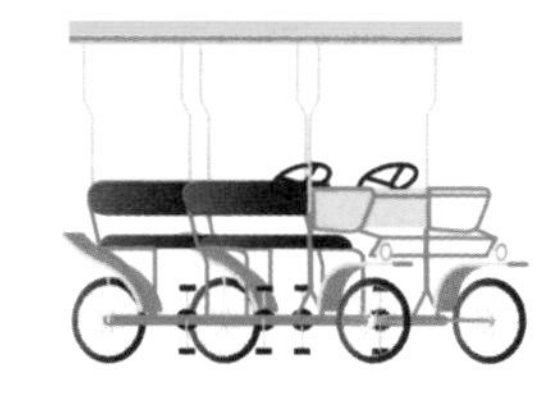
Pedicar

Punt

Paddle skateboard

Tricky terrain

4x4 pick-up truck

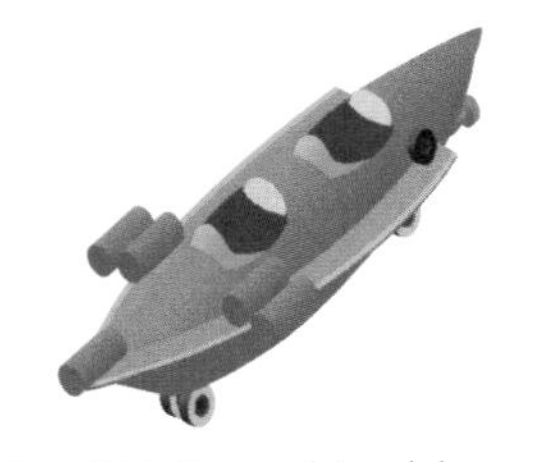
Amfibidiver drivable submarine

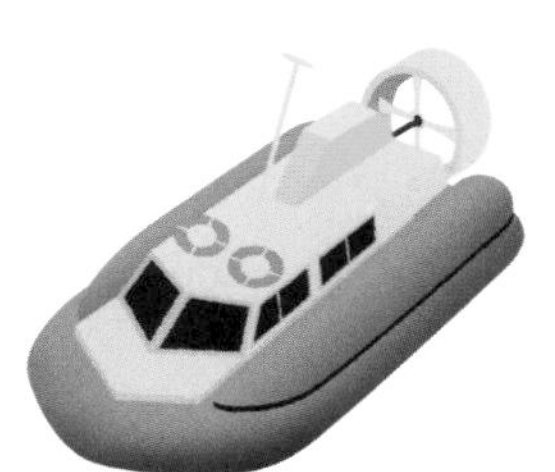
Hovercraft

Alligator amphibious tugboat

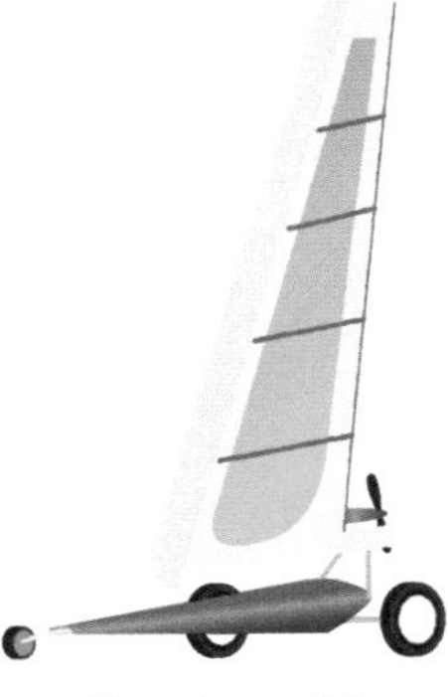
Sand yacht

Amphicar

Beach buggy

Dog sled

Dirt buggy

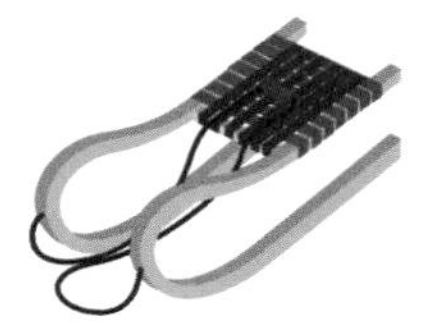
Sledge

Luge

Dune buggy

Float plane

Tundra buggy

Duck tour bus

Seated sled board

Sleigh

Snowblower truck

Dirt bike

Snow plough

Toboggan

Amfibus

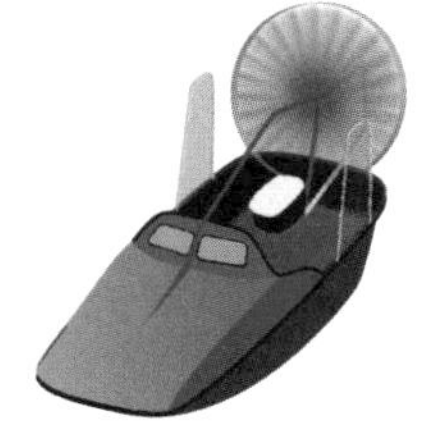
Hydrocopter

Swamp buggy

Hobbycar

Quad bike

All-terrain longboard

Sandmobile

Snowmobile

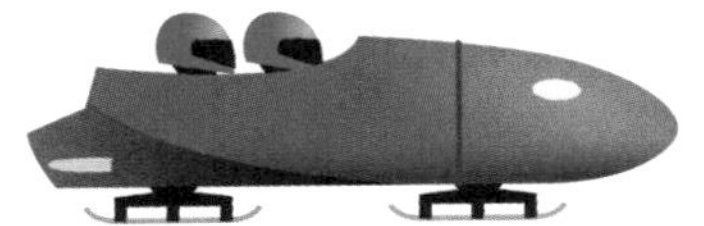
Bobsleigh

Snow coach

Screw-propelled vehicle

Snowplane

Trail bicycle

All-terrain vehicle

Rockets

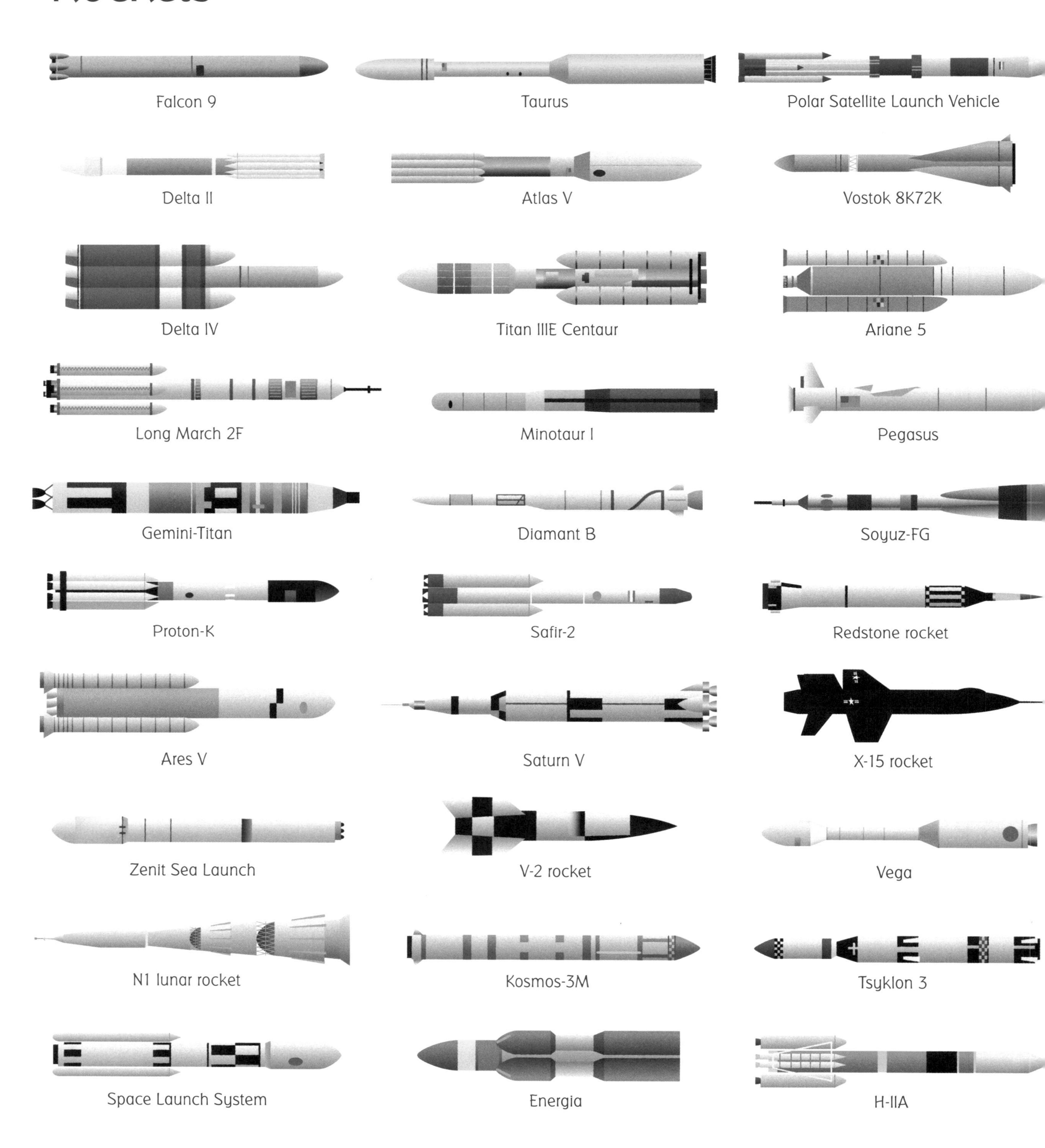
Falcon 9
Taurus
Polar Satellite Launch Vehicle
Delta II
Atlas V
Vostok 8K72K
Delta IV
Titan IIIE Centaur
Ariane 5
Long March 2F
Minotaur I
Pegasus
Gemini-Titan
Diamant B
Soyuz-FG
Proton-K
Safir-2
Redstone rocket
Ares V
Saturn V
X-15 rocket
Zenit Sea Launch
V-2 rocket
Vega
N1 lunar rocket
Kosmos-3M
Tsyklon 3
Space Launch System
Energia
H-IIA

In space

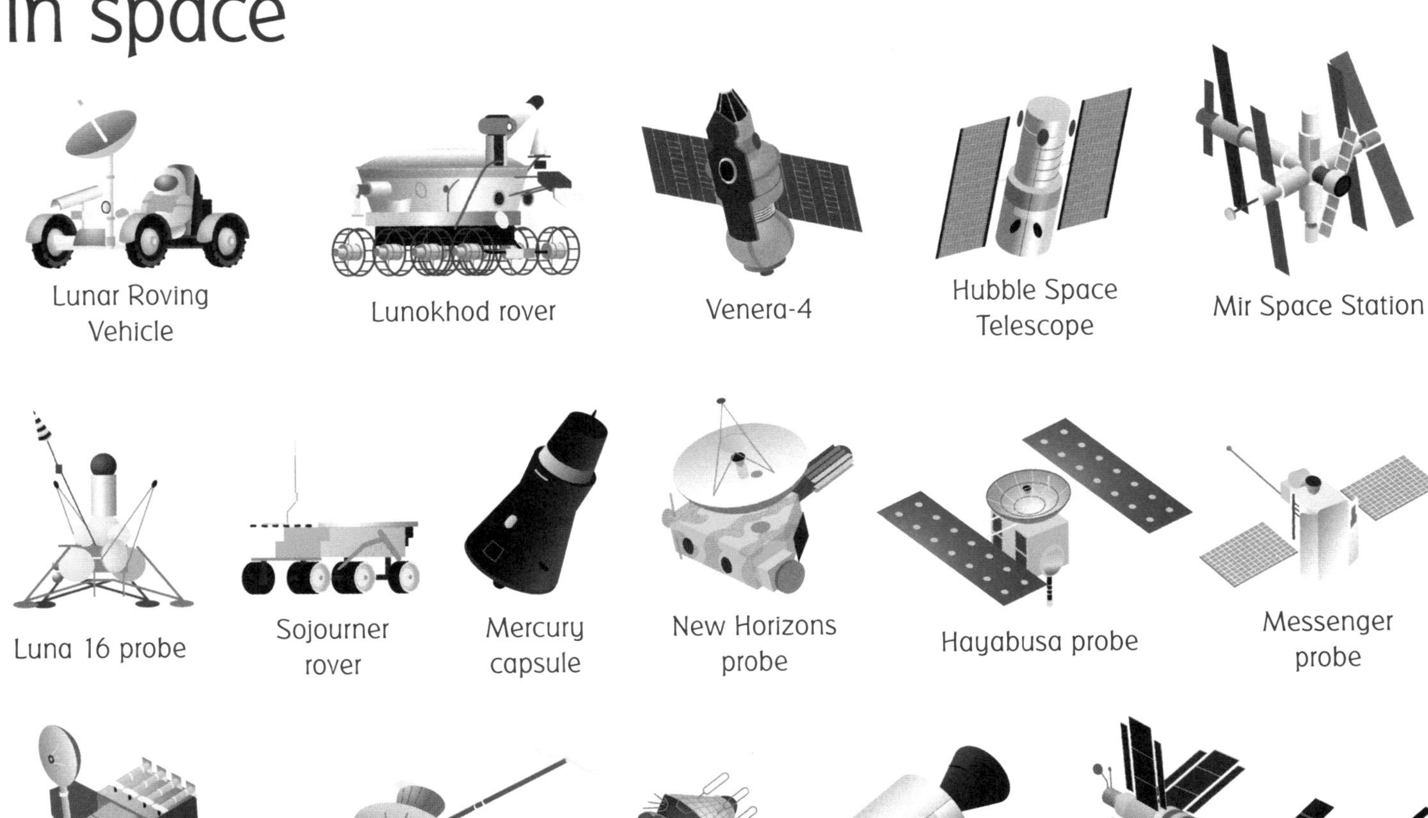

Lunar Roving Vehicle

Lunokhod rover

Venera-4

Hubble Space Telescope

Mir Space Station

Kepler telescope

Luna 16 probe

Sojourner rover

Mercury capsule

New Horizons probe

Hayabusa probe

Messenger probe

Opportunity rover

Solar Dynamics Observatory

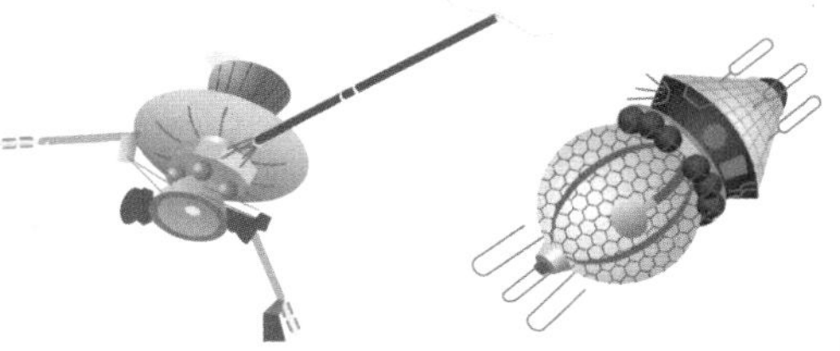

Galileo probe

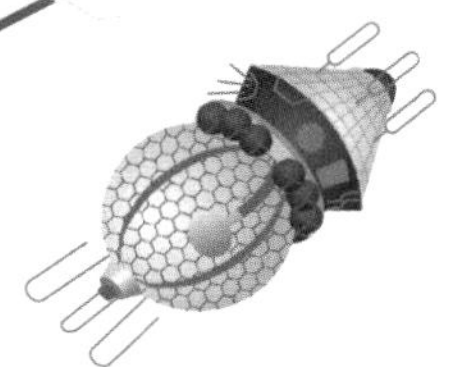

Vostok 1

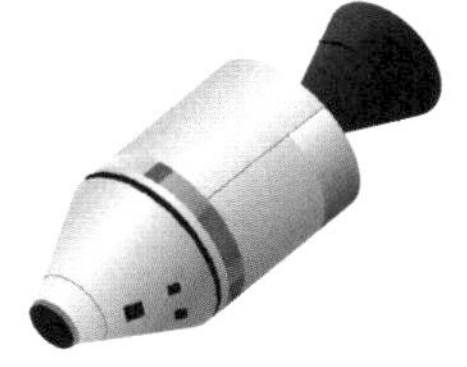

Columbia Command and Service Module

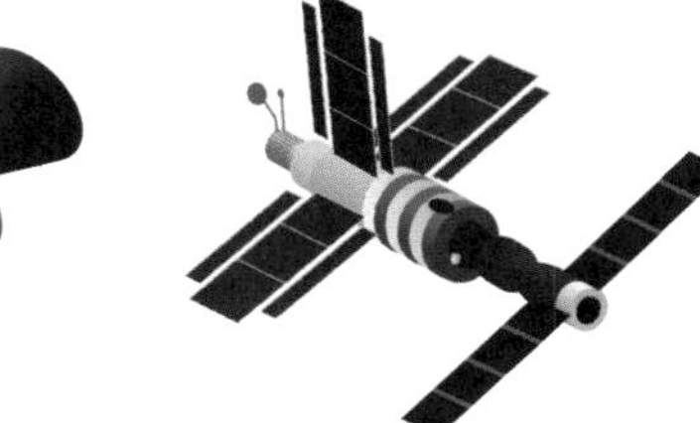

Salyut-7 Space Station

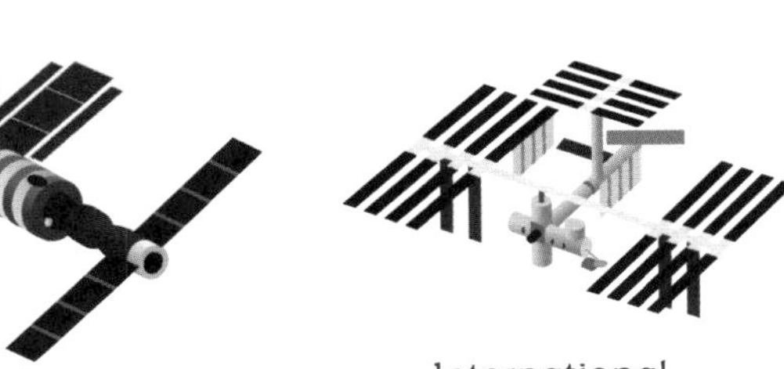

International Space Station

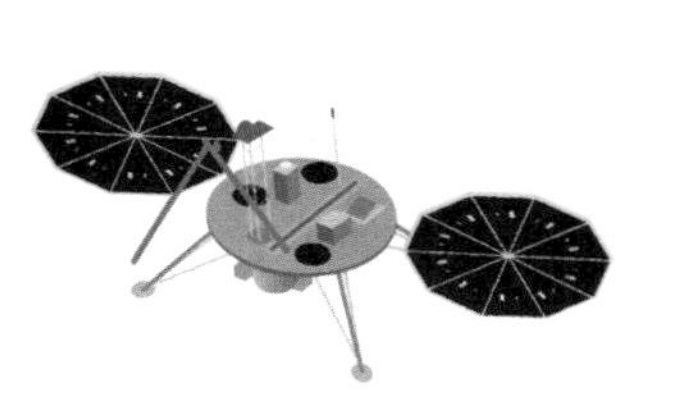

Phoenix Mars lander

Cassini probe

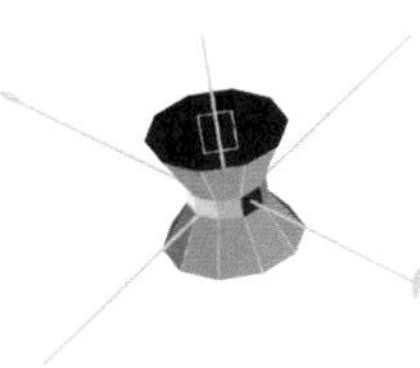

Helios probe

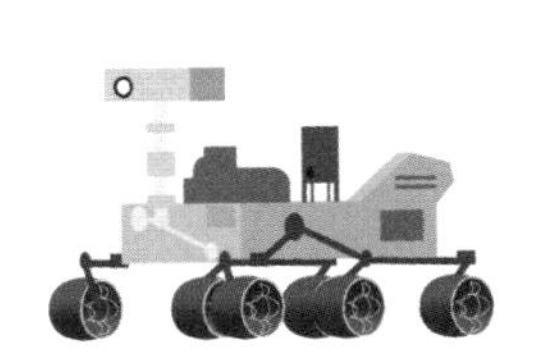

Curiosity rover

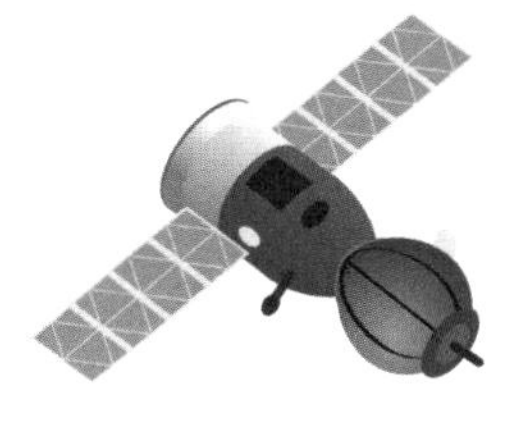

Soyuz spacecraft

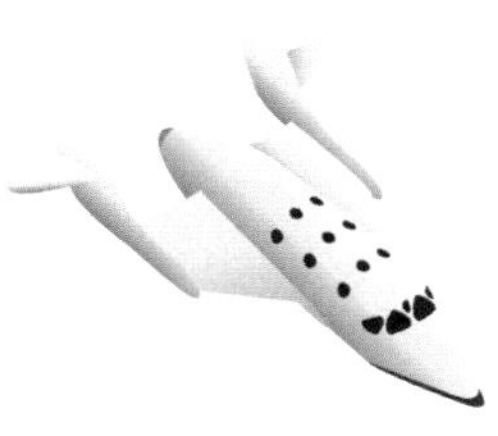

SpaceShipTwo

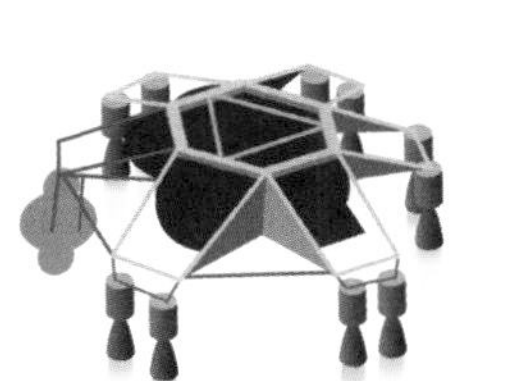

Mars sky crane

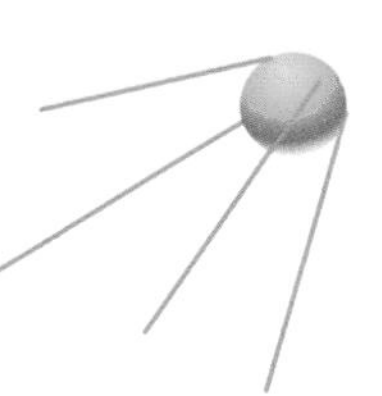

Sputnik 1

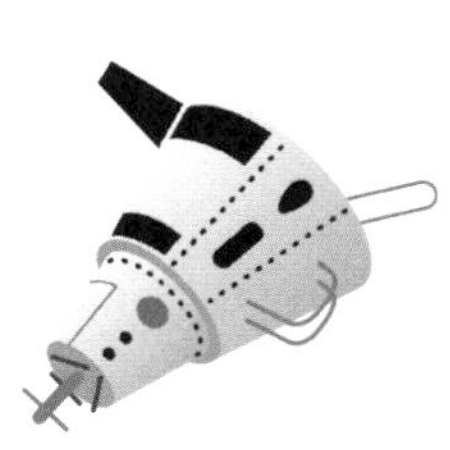

Sputnik 2

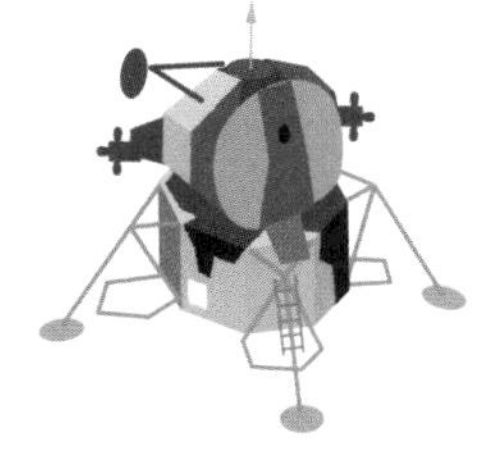

Eagle lunar module

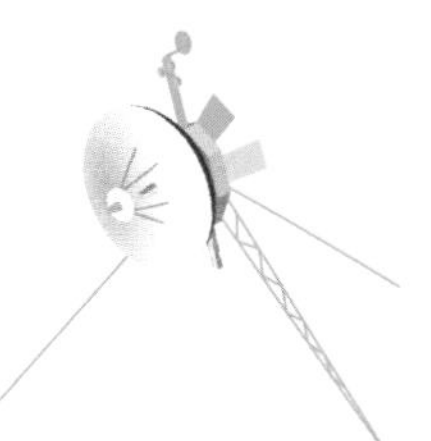

Voyager 1 probe

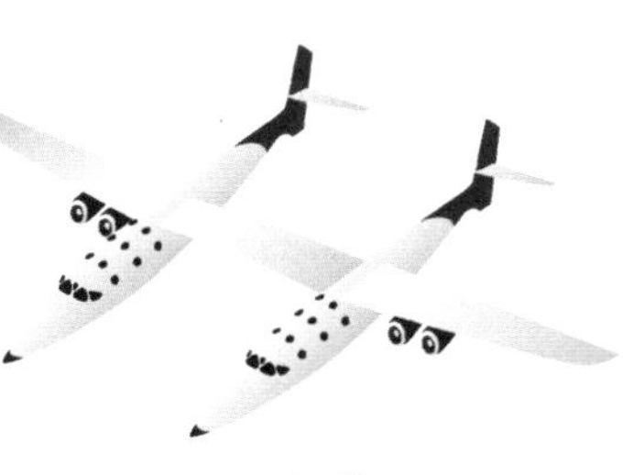

WhiteKnightTwo

NASA Space Shuttle

Luna 1

Viking 1 spacecraft

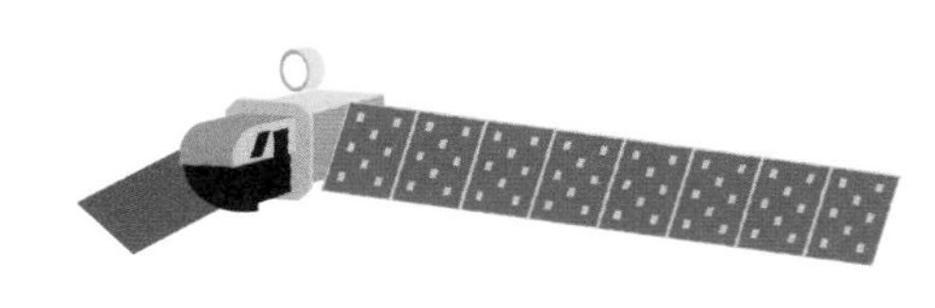

Earth observation satellite

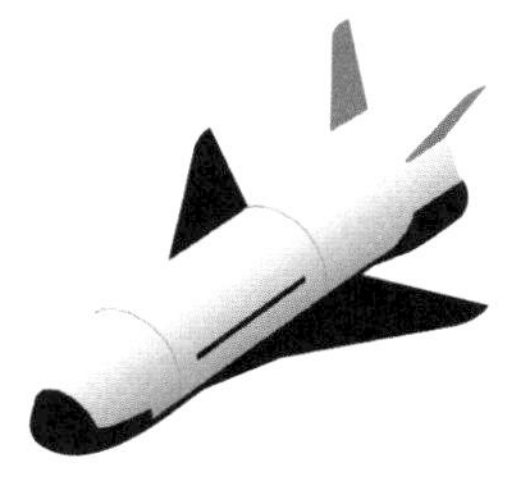

Orbital test vehicle

Unusual things that go

Index

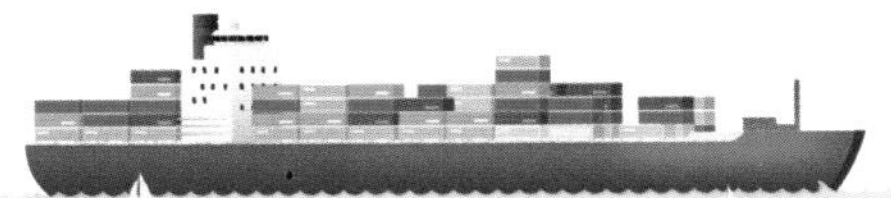

0-9
2-2-2 locomotive 25
3-door hatchback 9
4-4-2 locomotive 25
4x4 pick-up truck 28
5-door hatchback 9

A
Adler 25
Admiralty tug 19
Aerobatic plane 16
Aeroplanes 6, 7, 16, 17, 23, 24, 27, 28, 31
Aframax tanker 13
AH-1 Cobra 20
AH-64 Apache 20
Air ambulance 6
Air start unit 7
Aircraft carrier 19
Aircraft catering truck 7
Aircraft tug 7
Air-cushioned landing craft 19
Airport caddy 7
Airport fire appliance 7
Airport fuel truck 7
Airport maintenance truck 7
Airport shuttle train 7
Airside transfer bus 7
Alaskan land train 31
Albatros D.III 17
Allen scythe 23
Alligator amphibious tugboat 28
All-terrain fire vehicle 6
All-terrain longboard 28
All-terrain truck 22
All-terrain vehicle 28
Ambulance 6
Ambulance motorbike 6
Amfibidiver drivable submarine 28
Amfibus 28
Ammunition ship 19
Amphibious biplane 31
Amphicar 28
Antenna transporter 22
Ares V 29
Ariane 5 29
Armoured special forces vehicle 6
Articulated dump truck 21
Articulated locomotive 25
Articulated tugbarge 13
Asphalt paver 21
Atlas V 29
Auger excavator 20
Autogyro 16

B
B-1 Lancer 17
B-2 Spirit 'Stealth Bomber' 17
Backhoe loader 20
Backpack helicopter 31
Baggage truck 7
Baler 23
Ballast tamper 21
Ballistic missile submarine 19
Baltimore clipper 12
Banana board 27
Banana boat 8
Barque 12
Barquentine 12
Bass boat 15
Bathtub boat 15
Bathyscaphe 15
Battleship 19
Bawley 14
Beach buggy 28
Beach cruiser bicycle 27
Bean harvester 23
Bendy bus 5
Berlin U-Bahn train 5
Berliner helicopter 24
Bermudan sloop 14
Bicycle rickshaw 27
Bicycles 5, 6, 10, 24, 27, 28, 31
Big Boy 25
Big rig 22
Bike-share bicycle 5
Bilibili 15
Biplane 16
Black cab 5
Black Prince 18
Blackwall frigate 12
Blanchard's balloon 24
Blimp 16
Blood service car 6
Bluenose 11
BMX bicycle 27
Boarding stair truck 7
Boats 5, 6, 8, 10, 11, 12, 13, 14, 15, 19, 27, 28, 31
Bobber 11
Bobsleigh 28
Boda-boda bicycle 5
Bomb disposal vehicle 6
Boom truck 21
Bow rider 15
Boxcar 26
Bren Gun Carrier 18
Brig 12
Bristol Boxkite 24
Broadcast seeder 23
Brougham carriage 24
Bubble car 9
Bucentaur 12
Buckboard car 24
Bucket wheel excavator 20
Builder's van 21
Bulker 13
Bulldozer 20
Bullet train 26
Bumper car 8
Buses 5, 7, 8, 24, 27, 28, 31

C
Cab forward locomotive 25
Cabin motorcycle 11
Cable car 8
Cable layer 13
Caboose 26
Cabriolet 9
Café racer 11
Caïque 14
Camel bus 31
Camelback locomotive 25
Camper van 8
Canal boat 8
Cane train 26
Canoe 15
Car transporter 22
Caravan 8
Caravel 12
Cargo liner 13
Cargo loader 7
Cargo tram 26
Cars 5, 6, 7, 8, 9, 10, 24, 28, 31
Cassini probe 30
Catamaran 14
Catboat 14
Catering truck 22
Cat-ketch 14
Cave rescue vehicle 6
CH-47 Chinook 20
CH-54 Tarhe 20
Chain ferry 13
Chair lift 8
Challenger 1 18
Challenger 2 18
Challenger repair and recovery vehicle 18
Chariot 24
Charles' hydrogen balloon 24
Chemical tanker 13
Cherry picker 21
Chieftain bridgelayer 18
Child trailer 27
Child's tricycle 27
Chopper 11
Chopper-style bike 27
Churchill 18
Churchill Crocodile 18
Circus wagon 31
City car 9
City of Truro 25
Clarence carriage 24
Class 180 passenger train 26
Class 370 Advanced Passenger Train 26
Classic 1930s motorbike 11
Classic cabriolet 9
Classic car 9
Classic hot rod 10
Classic limousine 9
Clyde puffer 15
Coal box buggy 24
Coal face cutter 21
Coastguard boat 6
Coastguard helicopter 6
Coble 15
Cog 12
Cog railway 26
Columbia Command and Service Module 30
Combine harvester 23
Compact utility tractor 23
Concord stagecoach 24
Concrete mixer truck 21
Concrete pump truck 21
Condensing steam locomotive 25
Condor bomber 17
Conestoga wagon 24
Conference bicycle 27
Container ship 13
Container truck 22
Continuous miner 21
Coracle 15
Cornu helicopter 24
Corporate jet 7
Cotton picker 23
Coupé 9
Coxless four 10
Coxless pair 10
Crane ship 13
Crawler crane 21
Crawler tractor 23
Crop duster 23
Crop sprayer 23
Cross Channel ferry 13
Crossover 9
Crude oil tanker 13
Cruise ship 8
Cruiser motorbike 11
Cuddy boat 15
Cultivator 23
Curiosity rover 30
Currach 12
Curtainsider 22
Customs vehicle 7
Cutty Sark 11
Cyclo 5
Cyclocross bicycle 10

D
Daimler-Maybach motorcycle 24
Dassault Mirage III 17
Dassault Rafale C 17
Dazzle painted ship 19
Deep-submergence vehicle 15
De-icing truck 7
Dekochari art bicycle 27
Dekotora art truck 22
Delivery truck 22
Delivery van 5
Delta II 29
Delta IV 29
Derny 11
Devon lugger 14
Dhow 14
Diamant B 29
Diesel train 26
Diggers 20, 21, 24
Dirt bike 28
Dirt buggy 28
Dirt track racer motorbike 10
Disc harrow 23
Dog cart 24
Dog sled 28
Dornier Do-22 floatplane 17
Double-blade helicopter 16
Double-deck plane 7
Double-decker bus 5
Double-decker train 26
Double-decker tram 26
Double-drum roller 21
Dragline excavator 20
Dragon boat 10
Dragster 10
Dragster motorbike 10
Drascombe Drifter 14
Dray wagon 24
Dreadnought 19
Drillship 13
Dromond 12
Dropside truck 22
Dry bulk tanker 22
Dual sport motorbike 11
Duck tour bus 28
Dune buggy 28
Duplex locomotive 25

E
Eagle lunar module 30
Early oil-tanker 12
Earth observation satellite 30
Egyptian papyrus boat 12
Ekranoplan 31
Electric bicycle 5
Electric car 9
Electric diwheel 31
Electric motorbike 11
Electric rocket drag bike 11
Electric-steam locomotive 25
Elevating scraper 21
Ellehammer helicopter 24
Emergency doctor car 6
Emergency rescue ship 6
Enduro motorbike 11
Energia 29
Estate car 9
Eurofighter Typhoon 17
Eurostar 26
Express train 26

F
F-111 Aardvark 17
F-117 Nighthawk 17
F-14 Tomcat 17
F-15 Eagle 17
F-16 Fighting Falcon 17
F-18 Super Hornet 17
F-22 Raptor 17
F-35 Lightning II 17
F-4 Phantom 17
F4F Wildcat 17
F-86 Sabre jet 17
F9F Panther 17
Face-shovel 20
Factory trawler 13
Fairey Swordfish torpedo bomber 17
Fairy Queen Express 25
Falcon 9 29
Farm trailer 23
Farm truck 23
Farm wagon 24
Fast attack missile craft 19
Fast ferry 13
Fast goods locomotive 25
Feet first motorcycle 11
Feller buncher 21
Felucca 14
Fighter catapult ship 19
Fire boat 6
Fire motorbike 6
Fire truck 6
Fire-fighting helicopter 6
Fire-fighting water bomber 6
Fireless locomotive 25
Fishing boat 15
Flail mower 23
Flatbed truck 22
Flatboat 15
Flatcar 26
Fleet submarine 19
Flettner's rotor ship 13
Float plane 28
Float tube 15
Floating restaurant 8
Flo-flo ship 13
Fluyt 12
Flyak 15
Flying boat 16
Flying car 31
Flying hovercraft 31
Focke-Achgelis Fa 223 20
Fokker Eindecker 17
Folding bicycle 5
'Follow me' truck 7
Forage harvester 23
Forklift truck 21
Formula 1 car 10
Formula 3 car 10
Formula Ford car 10
Forwarder 21
Four-blade helicopter 16
Four-engined jet plane 7

Four-stack destroyer 19
Four-wheel drive 9
Freight bicycle 27
Freight ferry 13
Freight steam locomotive 25
Freight train 26
Friendship sloop 14
Front loader tractor 23
Front-entry cargo plane 7
Fuchs armoured personnel carrier 18
Fuel tanker 22
Funicular 26

G
Galileo probe 30
Galleass 12
Galleon 12
Garden tractor 23
Gas balloon 16
Gas tram 26
Gas turbine helicopter 16
Geared steam locomotive 25
Gemini-Titan 29
Giant crane 21
Giant loader 20
Giant tractor 23
Glider 16
Gloster Meteor 17
Go-fast boat 15
Golden Hind 11
Golf buggy 8
Gondola 27
GP2 car 10
Grab excavator 20
Grader 20
Grain cart 23
Grand Prix motorbike 10
Great Lakes freighter 13
Great Republic 11
Ground power unit 7
GT3 10
GT300 10
GT500 10
Guided missile destroyer 19
Gullwing car 9
Gully emptier 22
Gundalow 14
Gyrocar 31

H
H-IIA 29
H-13 Sioux 20
H-34 Choctaw 20
Handcar 27
Handcycle 27
Hang-glider 16
Hansom cab 24
Hardtop 9
Harvester 23
Hawker Hurricane 17
Hawker Siddeley Harrier 17
Hay tedder 23
Hayabusa probe 30
Heavy lift ship 13
Heavy muscle truck 22
Heilmann steam-electric locomotive 25
Heinkel bomber 17
Helicopters 6, 8, 16, 20, 24, 31
Helios probe 30
Helper locomotive 26
Hickman sea sled 12
High crop tractor 23
High-speed train 26
Highway maintenance truck 22
High-wing plane 16
Hire car 8
HMS Beagle 11
HMS Bounty 11
HMS Sovereign of the Seas 11
Hobbycar 28
Hobby-horse bicycle 24
Homebuilt aircraft 16
Hong Kong Mass Transit Railway train 5
Hop tug wagon 24
Hopper balloon 16
Horse van 23
Horse-drawn tram 26
Hospital ship 6
Hot air balloon 16
Hot hatch 9
Houseboat 15
Hovercraft 28
Howdah on elephant 31
Hubble Space Telescope 30
Human torpedo 19
Human-powered aircraft 27
Human-powered submarine 27
Humvee 18
Hybrid car 9
Hydro-bike 27
Hydrocopter 28
Hydrofoil 15
Hydrofoil scooter 8
Hydroplane 10

I
Ice boat 31
Ice cream van 8
Ice skates 8
Icebreaker 13
Indian auto-rickshaw 5
INDYCAR 10
Inflatable ringo 8
International Space Station 30
Interurban 26

J
Jet pack 31
Jet ski 8
Jetlev-flyer 31
Jetliner 7
John Bull 25
Jon boat 15
Jumbo jet 7
Junk 12
Junkers Ju-87 Stuka 17

K
KA-27 Helix 20
Kart 10
Kayak 15
Kei car 9
Kepler telescope 30
Ketch 14
Kick scooter 27
King Tiger 18
Kit car 9
Knarr 12
Kosmos-3M 29

L
La Pinta 11
Lancaster bomber 17
Land Walker exoskeleton 31
Landau carriage 24
Landing Vehicle Tracked 18
Laser dinghy 14
Lattice boom truck crane 22
Lavatory service vehicle 7
Le Mans classic car 9
Le Mans prototype 10
Lifeboat 6
Lifeguard boat 6
Lifeguard patrol vehicle 6
Light helicopter 16
Lighter barge 15
Light-sport aircraft 16
'Little Willie' 18
Littoral combat ship 19
Livestock truck 23
LNG tanker 13
Loader wagon 23
Logboat 15
Logging truck 22
London Underground train 5
Long March 2F 29
Long reach excavator 20
Longboard skateboard 27
Longtail boat 15
Longwall shearer 21
Low loader 21
Low-floor tram 26
Lowrider bicycle 27
Low-wing plane 16
Luge 28
Luna 1 30
Luna 16 probe 30
Lunar Roving Vehicle 30
Lunardi balloon 24
Lunokhod rover 30
Luxury car 9
Luxury yacht 8
Lynx Mk9A 20

M
M1 Abrams 18
M113 armoured personnel carrier 18
M2 Bradley 18
M3 half-track 18
M3 'Lee' 18
M4 Sherman 18
M728 combat engineer vehicle 18
Maglev train 26
Mail coach 24
Mail train 26
Mail truck 22
Mallard 25
Man-of-war 12
Manure spreader 23
Mark I 18
Mars sky crane 30
Mary Celeste 11
Mastiff patrol vehicle 18
Masula boat 15
Matatu 5
Mayflower 11
MD 500 Defender 20
Medium-lift helicopter 16
Merchant vessel 13
Mercury capsule 30
Merkava Mk4 18
Messenger probe 30
Mi-10 Harke 20
Mi-24 Hind 20
Micro scooter 27
Microcar 9
Microlight 16
Midget racer 10
Midget submarine 15
MiG-15 17
MiG-23 Flogger 17
Military vehicles 6, 17, 18, 19, 20
Milk tanker 22
Mines rescue vehicle 6
Minesweeper 19
Mini chopper 11
Mini excavator 20
Mini tractor 23
Miniature railway 26
Minibus 5
Mining train 26
Minotaur I 29
Mir Space Station 30
Mitsubishi A6M Zero 17
Mobile baggage conveyor 7
Mobile telescopic crane truck 22
Mobility scooter 5
Monitor ship 19
Monocycle 31
Monorail 26
Monster truck 22
Montgolfier balloon 24
Moped 5
Moscow Metro train 5
Motocross motorbike 10
Motor scooter 5
Motor yacht 15
Motorbikes 5, 6, 10, 11, 24, 31
Motorcycle trike 11
Motor-glider 16
Motorhome 8
Motorized monowheel 31
Motorsport rescue car 6
Mountain bicycle 27
Mountain rescue vehicle 6
Mtepe 12
Multi-purpose vehicle 9
Muscle car 9

N
N1 lunar rocket 29
Nao Victoria 11
Narrow tractor 23
NASA Space Shuttle 30
New Horizons probe 30
New York Subway train 5
Nordland boat 14
Norfolk wherry 14

O
Off-road racing truck 10
Offshore patrol vessel 19
OH-6 Cayuse 20
Omnibus 24
Open wagon 26
Open-top tour bus 8
Opportunity rover 30
Orange-crate scooter 27
Orbital test vehicle 30
Ornithopter 31
Out-front tractor mower 23
Outrigger canoe 15
Overhead train 26

P
P-26 'Peashooter' 17
P40 Carro Armato 18
P-40 Tomahawk 17
P-51 Mustang 17
P-61 Black Widow 17
Paddle skateboard 27
Paddle steamer 8
Paddlewheel canoe 31
Palace steamer 12
Pallet truck 21
Panamax ship 13
Panel truck 22
Panokseon 12
Panther command and liaison vehicle 18
Paris Metro train 5
Passenger lift 7
Passenger steamship 12
Patrol hydrofoil 19
Pedalo 8
Pedibus 27
Pedicar 27
Pegasus 29
Penny-farthing 24
Penteconter 12
Phillips Multiplane 24
Phoenix Mars lander 30
Pick-up truck 22
Piling rig 21
Pipe layer 21
Pipe-laying ship 13
Pirogue 15
Pizza delivery scooter 5
Planes 6, 7, 16, 17, 23, 24, 27, 28, 31
Platform supply vessel 13
Ploughing engine 24
Pocket bike 31
Pogo stick 27
Polar Satellite Launch Vehicle 29
Police bicycle 6
Police boat 6
Police dog van 6
Police helicopter 6
Police motorbike 6
Police patrol car 6
Police van 6
Pontoon 15
Portee truck 18
Porteur bicycle 27
Post driver 23
Post van 5
Potato planter 23
Potato spinner 23
Powerboat 10
Powered street luge 31
Powered wheelchair 5
Prairie schooner 24
Pram boat 15
Primary glider 16
Pro jet truck 10
Product tanker 13
Proton-K 29
Puffing Billy 25
Pump boat 15
Punt 27
Pusher aircraft 16

Q
Quad bike 28
Quadractor 31
Quadricycle 27
Quadrofoil 31
Quadski 31
Quinquereme 12

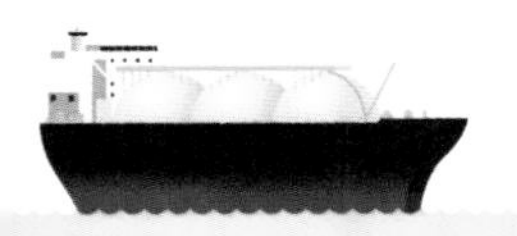

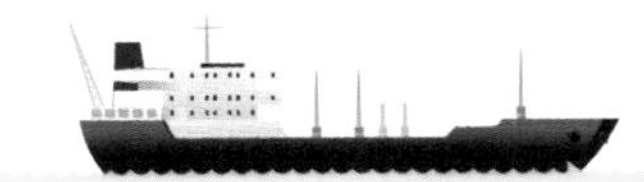

R
Race safety car 10
Racing shell 10
Racing sidecar 10
Racing sloop 10
Racing truck 10
Racing wheelchair 10
Racing yacht 10
Rack-and-pinion locomotive 25
Raft 15
Rally car 10
Range tracking ship 19
Rapid response ambulance car 6
Rat bike 11
Rat rod 10
Rear-entry cargo plane 7
Reclaimer 21
Recreational submarine 15
Recumbent bicycle 27
Redstone rocket 29
Reed boat 15
Refuelling tanker 16
Refuse collection truck 22
Regional jet 7
Rescue helicopter 6
Reversible tractor 23
Rigid dump truck 21
Rigid truck 22
Riverboat 8
RMS Titanic 11
Road planer 21
Road superbike 11
Roadheader 20
Roadster 9
Road-train 22
Roller skates 8
Rollerblades 8
Rollercoaster train 8
Roman galley 12
Roman merchant ship 12
Root crop harvester 23
Ro-pax ferry 13
Roper steam motorcycle 24
Rowing boat 27
Rozière balloon 16
Rubber dinghy 8
Rubber track tractor 23
Rubber-tyred Metro 26
Runway sweeper 7

S
SA-330 Puma 20
Sabot dinghy 14
Saddle tank locomotive 25
Safari vehicle 8
Safir-2 29
Sail wagon 24
Sailing tanker 31
Sailing yacht 15
Saloon car 9
Salyut-7 Space Station 30
Samaritan battlefield ambulance 18
Sampan 15
Sand yacht 28
Sandmobile 28
Saturn V 29
SBD Dauntless dive-bomber 17
School bus 5
Schooner 14
Scissor lift truck 22
Screw barque 12
Screw-propelled vehicle 28
Sculling boat 27
Sea Harrier 17
Sea tractor 31
Sea-going tram 31
Search and rescue vehicle 6
Seated sled board 28
Security vehicle 7
Seed drill 23
Segway PT 8
Self-loading concrete mixer 21
SH-3 Sea King 20
Shad boat 14
Sharpie boat 14
Shenyang J-8 Finback 17
Sherman Crab 18
Shikara 15
Ships 11, 12, 13, 19
Shuttle bus 7
Shuttle tanker 13
Side-entry cargo plane 7
Sideways bicycle 31
Sight-seeing helicopter 8
Site dumper 20
Site supervisor vehicle 21
Six-wheeled car 31
Six-wheeled tractor 23
Skateboard 27
Skerrie skiff 14
Skid steer loader 20
Skis 8
Sky crane 16
Sledge 28
Slegoon 31
Sleigh 28
Slipper launch 15
Small propeller plane 16
Small wheel bicycle 27
Snag boat 12
Snow coach 28
Snow plough 28
Snowblower truck 28
Snowboard 8
Snow-clearing truck 22
Snowmobile 28
Snowplane 28
Sociable bicycle 27
Soil compactor 21
Sojourner rover 30
Solar car 9
Solar Dynamics Observatory 30
Sopwith Camel 17
Soyuz spacecraft 30
Soyuz-FG 29
Space hopper 27
Space Launch System 29
Space Shuttle transporter truck 22
Spacecraft 29, 30
SpaceShipTwo 30
SPAD S.XIII 17
Special Operations Craft - 'Riverine' 19
Speedboat 8
Speedway motorbike 10
Sport bike 11
Sport touring bike 11
Sports car 9
Sputnik 1 30
Sputnik 2 30
SR-71 Blackbird 17
SS Central America 11
SS Savannah 11
Stealth corvette 19
Stealth ship 'Sea Shadow' 19
Steam car 24
Steam tractor 24
Steam yacht 12
Steamroller 24
Steamshovel 24
Stephenson's Rocket 25
Stockcar 10
Stourbridge Lion 25
Straight-decker 13
Streamliner motorcycle 11
Street bike 11
Street sweeper 5
Streetcar 5
Streetfighter bike 11
Stretch limousine 9
Stryker mobile gun system 18
Stunt car 31
Stunt helicopter 16
Stunt plane 31
Su-24 Fencer 17
Su-37 Terminator 17
Submarine rescue vehicle 6
Submersible watercraft 31
Submersibles 6, 15, 19, 27, 28, 31
Suction dredger 13
Suction excavator 20
Sugar cane harvester 23
Sukhoi Su-30 17
Super Guppy 31
Superbike 10
Supercar 9
Supercavitation boat 15
Supermarine Spitfire 17
Supermoto motorbike 10
Super-sized truck 22
Supersonic car 10
Supertanker 13
Surf rescue boat 6
Surface orbiter 31
Surfboard 8
Surrey carriage 24
Swamp buggy 28
Swan boat 8
Swather 23
Swing yarder 21
Sydney Harbour skiff 14
Syracusia 11

T
T-90 18
Tadpole trike 31
Tailless glider 16
Tandem 27
Tank wagon 26
Tanks 18
Tarai bune 15
Tartane 14
Taurus 29
Tejas Light Combat Aircraft 17
Telescopic handler 21
Thai tuk-tuk 5
The Empire State Express 25
The Flying Scotsman 25
The Glacier Express 26
The Kingston Flyer 25
The Leviathan 25
The Orient Express 26
Thermopylae 11
Three-engined jet plane 7
Three-wheel tractor 23
Three-wheeler 9
Threshing machine 24
Tilt rotor plane 16
Time-trial bicycle 10
Tipper truck 22
Titan IIIE Centaur 29
Tjotter 14
Toboggan 28
Tokyo Metro train 5
Tom Thumb 25
Tool-carrier tractor 23
Top fuel dragster 10
Topper 14
Torpedo boat 19
Tour coach 8
Touring bicycle 27
Touring car 10
Touring motorbike 11
Tow plane 16
Tow truck 22
Trabaccolo 14
Track bicycle 10
Track day car 9
Track skidder 21
Tracked excavator 20
Tracked scrap handler 21
Trackless train 8
Track-racing motorbike 10
Tractors 21, 23, 24, 31
Tractor-trailer 22
Traffic police car 6
Trail bicycle 28
Trailer cycle 27
Trains 5, 7, 8, 25, 26
Tram engine 26
Tramp steamer 12
Transparent canoe-kayak 31
Treadle bicycle 24
Trencher 20
Trevithick's locomotive 25
Trials bicycle 10
Triathlon bicycle 10
Trimaran 14
Trinity House tender 13
Trireme 12
Trisikad taxi 5
Trolley car 26
Trolleybus 24
Truck crane 21
Trucks 6, 7, 10, 18, 21, 22, 23, 28
Tsyklon 3 29
Tug 13
Tundra buggy 28
Tunnel boring machine 20
Turbinia 11
Turboprop plane 7
Turret ship 19
Turtle ship 12
Twin-engined plane 7
Twin-piston aircraft 7
Twin-rotor helicopter 16

U
U-boat 19
UH-1 Iroquois 20
UH-60 Black Hawk 20
UHT Tiger 20
Ultralight helicopter 16
Umiak 15
Underbone 11
Underground steam train 25
Unicycle 27
Universal Japanese motorcycle 11
Unlimited aerobatic glider 16
Utility bicycle 5
Utility helicopter 16
Utility landing craft 19

V
V-2 rocket 29
Van 5
Vans 5, 6, 8, 21, 23
Vector patrol vehicle 18
Vega 29
Velomobile 27
Venera-4 30
Vertical boiler locomotive 25
Very Slender Vessel 15
Veterinary ambulance 6
Vickers Gunbus FB5 17
Viking 1 spacecraft 30
Viking BVS10 18
Viking longship 12
Volocopter 31
Vostok 1 30
Vostok 8K72K 29
Voyager 1 probe 30

W
Wagonette 24
Waka 15
Wakeboard 8
Walking tractor 23
Warrior armoured vehicle 18
Warthog armoured vehicle 18
Waste disposal truck 5
Water ski boat 8
Water skis 8
Water taxi 5
Wave board 27
Wayfarer dinghy 14
Wheel tractor-scraper 21
Wheelchair 27
Wheeled excavator 20
Wheeled loader 20
Wheeled scrap handler 21
WhiteKnightTwo 30
Windsurfing board 8
Wishbone ketch 14
Wolfhound patrol vehicle 18
Wood-powered El Camino 31
World War I cruiser 19
World War II destroyer 19
Wrecker truck 21
Wright Flyer III 24

X
X-15 rocket 29
X-bow support ship 13

Y
Yarder 21
Yawl 14
Yellow taxi 5

Z
Zenit Sea Launch 29
Zeppelin 16
Zip-line 8
Zorbing ball 31

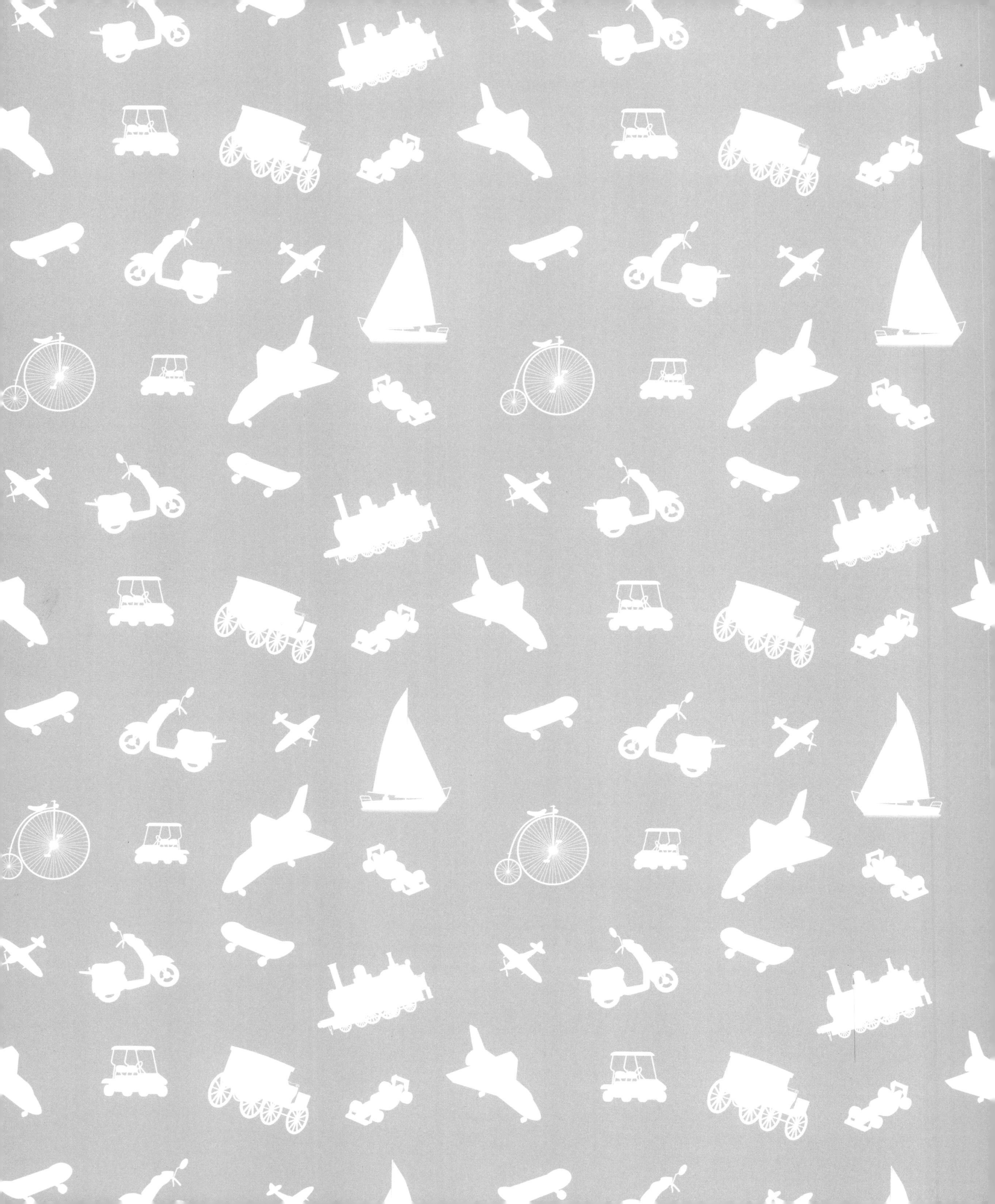